SELMA EVANS

ADHD TOOLKIT FOR ADULTS

Effective Strategies for Overcoming ADHD Challenges: Enhance Focus, Confidence and Boost Your Productivity and Wellbeing

ISBN: 979-12-81498-07-5

TABLE OF CONTENTS

INTRODUCTION — 1

CHAPTER 1: WHAT IS ADHD? — 5

CHAPTER 2: THE INFLUENCE OF ADHD ON SOCIAL INTERACTIONS — 13

CHAPTER 3: VARIOUS FORMS OF ADHD — 21

CHAPTER 4: FACTORS CONTRIBUTING TO ADHD — 27

CHAPTER 5: IDENTIFYING ADHD: A GUIDE TO DIAGNOSIS — 31

CHAPTER 6: ADDRESSING ADHD: APPROACHES TO TREATMENT — 43

CHAPTER 7: ADHD MANAGEMENT THROUGH BEHAVIORAL THERAPY — 49

CHAPTER 8: BOOSTING MEMORY ABILITIES FOR PEOPLE WITH ADHD — 57

CHAPTER 9: CONQUERING YOUR WEAKNESSES — 74

CHAPTER 10: MANAGING ANXIETY-INDUCING WORKPLACE SITUATIONS — 83

CHAPTER 11: ADULT ADHD AND ITS IMPACT ON ROMANTIC RELATIONSHIPS — 96

CHAPTER 12: COPING WITH LOW MOOD AND DE-
PRESSION ... 111

CHAPTER 13: DIET AND PHYSICAL ACTIVITY TO EN-
HANCE FOCUS AND MANAGE EMOTIONS ... 127

CHAPTER 14: CONQUERING ADHD CHALLENGES ... 131

CHAPTER 15: ESSENTIAL KNOWLEDGE TO OVER-
COME ADHD ... 136

CHAPTER 16: GETTING THE RIGHT HELP AND SUP-
PORT ... 145

CHAPTER 17: ASSISTING OTHERS IN MANAGING
ADHD ... 152

CONCLUSION ... 155

INTRODUCTION

The best way to deal with the symptoms of Attention Deficit Hyperactivity Disorder is to learn strategies for self-management. Focusing on what works for you will help you express your ADHD successfully in school and at work. This workbook is designed with that goal in mind, providing long-term solutions that can be implemented in your everyday life.

Everyone is different. ADHD is a neurobiological condition that affects people differently, depending on their genetic background and other factors. The strategies presented in this workbook are based on verified information from studies of children and adults with ADHD, as well as from my own experiences as a person with ADHD.

ADHD is a hidden disability that usually goes undiagnosed and untreated, but it can be managed effectively. This workbook contains proven strategies for self-management in the workplace, at school, and in social situations. It emphasizes the need to practice these strategies daily to reinforce new patterns of behavior.

Have you ever felt misunderstood? Like nobody really knows how you feel and what you're going through? I've heard stories from people with ADHD who have been insulted or even disowned by their own family members because they believed they weren't trying hard enough.

This is about more than just learning how to get organized, pay attention in class, or wait your turn. It's about understanding the world you live in and your place in it. You deserve an equal chance at success, and this workbook is part of that journey.

As an adult with ADHD, you may never have had the opportunity to solve the problems you face on a daily basis. You may feel foolish or embarrassed about things that come naturally to others. You may think that these problems are your fault and that there's no one who can help you manage your life. But now there is help.

This book will help you through the challenges of ADHD adult life.

This workbook is primarily focused on self-management. It will teach you how to organize yourself, be more productive, and solve problems. It also will provide helpful strategies for dealing with the consequences of living with ADHD.

You will learn strategies for self-management based on ADHD science, and some personal experiences of young adults with ADHD. You will learn how to identify, treat, and even prevent ADHD symptoms. You will also learn strategies for long-term support through adulthood and a discussion of the most important challenges you may face.

You're a person, just like everyone else. And you have a disorder, just like many other people. Your actions have consequences, both good and bad. This workbook is designed to help and understand the world you live in so you can respond better to it. You are the one person who is in charge of your actions. Now is the time for you to take control.

This book will help you achieve greater self-awareness and improve your ability to lead a more fulfilling life. My hope is that these strategies help you manage stress, increase self-esteem, build better relationships, and have fun with friends. Most of these strategies are easy to learn and can last a lifetime.

If you have ADHD, you are not alone. You are part of a large community of people with ADHD who are trying to live productive, fulfilling lives. If your family members, friends, teachers, or employers have treated you unfairly because you have ADHD or because they do not understand it—take heart! You are the only person responsible for your actions.

You have the power to get organized, learn new strategies for self-management, and get on with your life. It's not too late to make changes for the better.

Maybe your mind wanders frequently when you're trying to pay attention in class. Or maybe you have trouble getting started on a task. Or maybe you're easily distracted. Perhaps you get frustrated when things don't go your way. Perhaps you feel bored and restless all the time. For some people, these and similar problems may be part of the new challenges of adult life: You may have learned to cope with life's challenges by using medication, but now your body is telling you it's time to take new steps to manage your condition.

Whatever your experience with ADHD has been, this workbook will help you understand who you are and how to live well. It emphasizes what you need to know about ADHD and how the disorder affects you. It also emphasizes what you can do to live well with ADHD.

Everyone is different, and each of us have unique stories to tell. I hope that by reading about the experiences of other people in this workbook, you will gain insight into your own life. You can use these strategies to help you improve your life, improve your relationships with others, and make every day count.

You are unique, but you are not alone. There is hope. Millions of people like you live and work successfully with ADHD every day, while living productive and satisfying lives.

I know it's hard to make reasonable choices when you feel overwhelmed or frustrated by daily challenges. You may want to avoid some certain situations or people, but that choice rarely prevents you from dealing with the situation in the best way possible.

I encourage you to think of yourself as a unique person with ADHD, not someone who is broken or defective. There is nothing wrong with you. It is the way your brain works that makes you different. And it's our differences that make this world a more interesting place for everyone, including yourself.

My goal is to help you increase your awareness of yourself, today and in the future. When you are aware of yourself, you have a better chance of succeeding in the choices you make.

CHAPTER 1: WHAT IS ADHD?

A DHD stands for Attention Deficit Hyperactivity Disorder. It is a chronic medical condition characterized by three main types of symptoms: inattention, hyperactivity, and impulsivity. ADHD is one of the most popular behavioral disorders among children. Although ADHD is most commonly diagnosed in children, it can also be diagnosed in adults, particularly if they are struggling with irregular attention spans or exhibit hyperactivity. Many people with ADHD also experience problems regulating their emotions and may show signs of depression. This is because ADHD impacts areas of the brain that are responsible for managing emotions.

Because ADHD is a genetic disorder, it can be passed on from parent to child. Children who have one parent with ADHD will more than likely be affected by the disorder. ADHD is more prevalent in boys than girls. This is believed to be because males have a more difficult time controlling their impulses and emotions, which can lead to behavioral issues. A person's life may also be impacted by the disorder: if left untreated, it can lead to poor school performance and relationship problems. Finally, there is evidence that ADHD may cause other mental disorders such as depression and anxiety.

People with ADHD may experience extreme difficulty concentrating, and hyperactivity. This often causes problems in school and other social situations.

While we don't fully understand the causes of ADHD, one theory points to hyperactivity as a way to fight off fear to protect the body from overwhelming stress. Studying the brains of children with ADHD has shown that there are many changes in the frontal lobe – the area of the brain responsible for controlling emotions.

The prefrontal cortex, the area of the brain involved with emotions, is significantly smaller in those with ADHD. Researchers think that this results from a drop in levels of dopamine, a chemical that is responsible for controlling emotions. According to one theory, the mild damage caused by ADHD during childhood causes lower dopamine levels to persist into adulthood.

This will cause less control over emotions, as well as difficulty concentrating, and being hyperactive.

ADHD isn't going away. It's a part of the human condition that will likely continue throughout your life. Improvements in understanding and treatment will likely occur in time, but it's important to remember that people with ADHD are often misunderstood and treated unfairly.

People with ADHD often feel helpless. They feel as if they are broken somehow, which can lead to depression.

People with ADHD often experience emotional and physical problems as a result of their condition. They may feel overwhelmed and depressed by the challenges they face and may have trouble enjoying life: they might feel restless, irritable, and impatient. They could also suffer from headaches, stomach aches, or sleeping problems.

ADHD is like having a short fuse. People with ADHD may become bored extremely quickly. They give up easily if they think something is hard or not worth the effort to learn. They are often impulsive; thus, they may blurt out rude comments without thinking about the consequences.

On the other hand, individuals with ADHD may appear to be always on the go and have a prodigious work ethic. Many people with ADHD have been successful in careers that require them to work independently with little supervision, such as writing or computer programming.

A diagnosis of ADHD does not mean that someone is unintelligent or that he is a bad student. In fact, most people with ADHD have above-average intelligence. However, they may have difficulty applying what they know to ensure consistent good grades in school.

Teachers need to understand that students with ADHD are not lazy or trying to be disruptive. Some teachers may unfairly expect students with ADHD to have the same focus and attention span as their other students. Many adults with ADHD are frustrated because they think they are "lazy" or "dumb." They cannot concentrate for very long, no matter how much they try.

Neurobiological and genetic concepts

There are strong familial links between ADHD and psychiatric comorbidities such as bipolar disorder, generalized anxiety disorder, and major depressive disorder. This doesn't mean you would automatically have these disorders if your parents had them, but it means that these problems might be more likely than in the general population.

The three main neurotransmitters in the brain—dopamine, norepinephrine and serotonin—play an important role in ADHD. Research shows that 60 percent of children with ADHD have a deficit in one or another of these neurotransmitters.

The pathways for these neurotransmitters are also connected to other systems in the brain involving executive function, impulse control, attention, language, memory, learning and emotion. A deficit in these areas can contribute to problems with self-control or impulsivity.

It is also important to recognize that ADHD can vary in presentation, severity and symptoms across the life cycle. For example, inattention is the major symptom of ADHD during childhood, but hyperactivity or impulsivity may be more prominent in adulthood. Likewise, impairment in one's ability to plan ahead and resist temptation may become more severe during adolescence than it was during childhood.

Because everyone with ADHD has a unique set of symptoms that can change over time, each person requires an individualized approach to treatment that will address these changes. This is why a comprehensive treatment plan will include medication, psychosocial therapy and family support.

In addition to the core symptoms of inattention and hyperactivity/impulsivity, the disorder is often characterized by coexisting problems in several areas, including:

- Relationship difficulties

- Poor self-esteem

- Mood disorders

- Anxiety disorders

- Learning disabilities

- Conduct disorder or oppositional defiant disorder (ODD) in adulthood.

The symptoms of ADHD are frequently misunderstood. For example, it is common for someone to say that a problem or difference in an adult "is just part of who I am and how I was raised." Or the condition might be called a "personality trait."

It can also be extremely frustrating to be made fun of and teased by peers, even though the individual is not able to control his or her behavior. This can lead people with ADHD to become withdrawn and isolated as they get older.

ADHD is not flaw or a personality disorder, but it has some strong similarities. The main difference is that ADHD is not caused by poor parenting or other uncontrollable forces, but rather by a biological predisposition to have trouble with attention and hyperactivity.

ADHD in adults

It is commonly believed that adults who had behavioral problems as children will have the same problems as adults. In reality, some people with ADHD grow out of their symptoms, while others do not.

If you suspect you might have ADHD, it's important to know that many adults can live successful lives despite the challenges of this disorder.

Most adults with ADHD are not hyperactive. If your biggest complaint is that you are very forgetful, easily distracted or disorganized, then you might be an adult with ADHD who has outgrown your hyperactivity.

Behavioral problems in children more often reflect the effects of environmental factors than they do a biological condition. However, ADHD is not a character flaw and there is no proof that the disorder will lead to poor adult outcomes.

Effect of ADHD on family

Adults with ADHD are not the only ones who are affected by this disorder. Friends, parents, siblings, grandparents, and other relatives are also affected. It is common for the family to live under stress because of this disorder. Emotional and behavioral problems like mood swings, chronic lateness, and trouble concentrating can cause problems in the family.

Adults with ADHD may also cause anxiety to their families. They often feel remorse over the problems they cause their families through their actions or behavior. They become aware of the effects it has on their families, but because the condition makes it difficult for them to control themselves, they can't change. This is why adults with ADHD have a tendency to avoid social or family gatherings. They often feel embarrassed and uncomfortable in the presence of their families.

Family problems that are common in adults with ADHD are often due to lack of communication. Adults with ADHD often do not allow for constructive criticism, or try to involve their families in their daily activities. They feel embarrassed when they make mistakes and show emotion, like tears or anger. These emotional upsets put more pressure on the family, causing them to avoid social gatherings altogether. Adults with ADHD are often a cause of stress to their families because they are emotionally unstable. This can cause some families to break.

Adults with ADHD are often unhappy with their families because the disorder makes it hard for them to have a good relationship. They have problems maintaining close relationships. This is because adults with ADHD often do not understand the feelings of others, and they don't know how to talk about their own feelings or problems.

Adults with ADHD often don't correct their children when they do things wrong or when their behavior is inappropriate. Children usually learn these behaviors from their parents because the parents set bad examples for them to follow. This can cause more problems for the family.

Having ADHD also affects the family physically. Family members may get sick because they become part of the daily struggles that adults with ADHD go through. The problems can also affect the family economically. It is difficult for adults with ADHD to be involved in financial matters or take care of their family finances. They often lose jobs, get fired frequently, and have trouble doing their jobs adequately because of their unpredictable behavior.

In order to avoid damaging their family, adults with ADHD need to learn how to control their behavior and mannerisms in order to be able to lead a normal and healthy life. Their families may also need assistance in dealing with their problems and understanding how they can help their loved one rather than complaining about the daily struggles of the adult with ADHD.

Effects on Society

An individual with ADHD has difficulty learning social skills, like how to get along with others, deal with feelings, express opinions, solve problems cohesively and communicate. This disability can cause the person to be isolated from society. Adults with ADHD may have trouble getting along with others because they are unable to understand others' feelings, perspectives and motivations. They also may not be able to see or understand the differences between their own behaviors and those of others. They may not even know how to express their feelings, and may not be aware of how their behavior affects others.

The behavior of those with ADHD can also lead to an increased risk of accidents that could cause harm to them or others around them. It has been reported that adults with ADHD are involved in more accidents than others, particularly on the road. This is because the symptoms of ADHD affect their driving skills. Adults with ADHD have a greater tendency to be involved in traffic accidents because of their impulsive behavior and short attention span. Moreover, they do not know how to properly react when encountering a dangerous situation on the road. It makes them more vulnerable to injury and death in car crashes.

ADHD has been found to have a negative impact on the economy due to the decrease in productivity and loss of working hours. Adults with ADHD are often unable to do their designated tasks. This results in them being absent from work, losing their jobs, and having trouble maintaining their job performance. The resulting decrease in productivity reduces the revenue of society as a whole, which can result in higher unemployment rates.

Adults with ADHD may also become involved in crime due to their inability to control their behaviors and anger. This lack of self-control makes it hard for them to stay out of trouble, especially when they get angry.

They also may take part in problematic behavior like alcoholism and eating disorders. They drink too much and take in large amounts of food to feel comfort and forget about their troubles. Both problems can lead to even more serious problems, like violence, smoking, and drug abuse.

CHAPTER 2: THE INFLUENCE OF ADHD ON SOCIAL INTERACTIONS

ADHD stands for Attention Deficit Hyperactivity Disorder. It is a chronic medical condition characterized by three main types of symptoms: inattention, hyperactivity, and impulsivity. ADHD is one of the most popular behavioral disorders among children. Although ADHD is most commonly diagnosed in children, it can also be diagnosed in adults, particularly if they are struggling with irregular attention spans or exhibit hyperactivity. Many people with ADHD also experience problems regulating their emotions and may show signs of depression. This is because ADHD impacts areas of the brain that are responsible for managing emotions.

Because ADHD is a genetic disorder, it can be passed on from parent to child. Children who have one parent with ADHD will more than likely be affected by the disorder. ADHD is more prevalent in boys than girls. This is believed to be because males have a more difficult time controlling their impulses and emotions, which can lead to behavioral issues. A person's life may also be impacted by the disorder: if left untreated, it can lead to poor school performance and relationship problems. Finally, there is evidence that ADHD may cause other mental disorders such as depression and anxiety.

People with ADHD may experience extreme difficulty concentrating, and hyperactivity. This often causes problems in school and other social situations.

While we don't fully understand the causes of ADHD, one theory points to hyperactivity as a way to fight off fear to protect the body from overwhelming stress. Studying the brains of children with ADHD has shown that there are many changes in the frontal lobe – the area of the brain responsible for controlling emotions.

The prefrontal cortex, the area of the brain involved with emotions, is significantly smaller in those with ADHD. Researchers think that this results from a drop in levels of dopamine, a chemical that is responsible for controlling emotions. According to one theory, the mild damage caused by ADHD during childhood causes lower dopamine levels to persist into adulthood.

This will cause less control over emotions, as well as difficulty concentrating, and being hyperactive.

ADHD isn't going away. It's a part of the human condition that will likely continue throughout your life. Improvements in understanding and treatment will likely occur in time, but it's important to remember that people with ADHD are often misunderstood and treated unfairly.

People with ADHD often feel helpless. They feel as if they are broken somehow, which can lead to depression.

People with ADHD often experience emotional and physical problems as a result of their condition. They may feel overwhelmed and depressed by the challenges they face and may have trouble enjoying life: they might feel restless, irritable, and impatient. They could also suffer from headaches, stomach aches, or sleeping problems.

ADHD is like having a short fuse. People with ADHD may become bored extremely quickly. They give up easily if they think something is hard or not worth the effort to learn. They are often impulsive; thus, they may blurt out rude comments without thinking about the consequences.

On the other hand, individuals with ADHD may appear to be always on the go and have a prodigious work ethic. Many people with ADHD have been successful in careers that require them to work independently with little supervision, such as writing or computer programming.

A diagnosis of ADHD does not mean that someone is unintelligent or that he is a bad student. In fact, most people with ADHD have above-average intelligence. However, they may have difficulty applying what they know to ensure consistent good grades in school.

Teachers need to understand that students with ADHD are not lazy or trying to be disruptive. Some teachers may unfairly expect students with ADHD to have the same focus and attention span as their other students. Many adults with ADHD are frustrated because they think they are "lazy" or "dumb." They cannot concentrate for very long, no matter how much they try.

Neurobiological and genetic concepts

There are strong familial links between ADHD and psychiatric comorbidities such as bipolar disorder, generalized anxiety disorder, and major depressive disorder. This doesn't mean you would automatically have these disorders if your parents had them, but it means that these problems might be more likely than in the general population.

The three main neurotransmitters in the brain—dopamine, norepinephrine and serotonin—play an important role in ADHD. Research shows that 60 percent of children with ADHD have a deficit in one or another of these neurotransmitters.

The pathways for these neurotransmitters are also connected to other systems in the brain involving executive function, impulse control, attention, language, memory, learning and emotion. A deficit in these areas can contribute to problems with self-control or impulsivity.

It is also important to recognize that ADHD can vary in presentation, severity and symptoms across the life cycle. For example, inattention is the major symptom of ADHD during childhood, but hyperactivity or impulsivity may be more prominent in adulthood. Likewise, impairment in one's ability to plan ahead and resist temptation may become more severe during adolescence than it was during childhood.

Because everyone with ADHD has a unique set of symptoms that can change over time, each person requires an individualized approach to treatment that will address these changes. This is why a comprehensive treatment plan will include medication, psychosocial therapy and family support.

In addition to the core symptoms of inattention and hyperactivity/impulsivity, the disorder is often characterized by coexisting problems in several areas, including:

- Relationship difficulties

- Poor self-esteem

- Mood disorders

- Anxiety disorders

- Learning disabilities

- Conduct disorder or oppositional defiant disorder (ODD) in adulthood.

The symptoms of ADHD are frequently misunderstood. For example, it is common for someone to say that a problem or difference in an adult "is just part of who I am and how I was raised." Or the condition might be called a "personality trait."

It can also be extremely frustrating to be made fun of and teased by peers, even though the individual is not able to control his or her behavior. This can lead people with ADHD to become withdrawn and isolated as they get older.

ADHD is not flaw or a personality disorder, but it has some strong similarities. The main difference is that ADHD is not caused by poor parenting or other uncontrollable forces, but rather by a biological predisposition to have trouble with attention and hyperactivity.

ADHD in adults

It is commonly believed that adults who had behavioral problems as children will have the same problems as adults. In reality, some people with ADHD grow out of their symptoms, while others do not.

If you suspect you might have ADHD, it's important to know that many adults can live successful lives despite the challenges of this disorder.

Most adults with ADHD are not hyperactive. If your biggest complaint is that you are very forgetful, easily distracted or disorganized, then you might be an adult with ADHD who has outgrown your hyperactivity.

Behavioral problems in children more often reflect the effects of environmental factors than they do a biological condition. However, ADHD is not a character flaw and there is no proof that the disorder will lead to poor adult outcomes.

Effect of ADHD on family

Adults with ADHD are not the only ones who are affected by this disorder. Friends, parents, siblings, grandparents, and other relatives are also affected. It is common for the family to live under stress because of this disorder. Emotional and behavioral problems like mood swings, chronic lateness, and trouble concentrating can cause problems in the family.

Adults with ADHD may also cause anxiety to their families. They often feel remorse over the problems they cause their families through their actions or behavior. They become aware of the effects it has on their families, but because the condition makes it difficult for them to control themselves, they can't change. This is why adults with ADHD have a tendency to avoid social or family gatherings. They often feel embarrassed and uncomfortable in the presence of their families.

Family problems that are common in adults with ADHD are often due to lack of communication. Adults with ADHD often do not allow for constructive criticism, or try to involve their families in their daily activities. They feel embarrassed when they make mistakes and show emotion, like tears or anger. These emotional upsets put more pressure on the family, causing them to avoid social gatherings altogether. Adults with ADHD are often a cause of stress to their families because they are emotionally unstable. This can cause some families to break.

Adults with ADHD are often unhappy with their families because the disorder makes it hard for them to have a good relationship. They have problems maintaining close relationships. This is because adults with ADHD often do not understand the feelings of others, and they don't know how to talk about their own feelings or problems.

Adults with ADHD often don't correct their children when they do things wrong or when their behavior is inappropriate. Children usually learn these behaviors from their parents because the parents set bad examples for them to follow. This can cause more problems for the family.

Having ADHD also affects the family physically. Family members may get sick because they become part of the daily struggles that adults with ADHD go through. The problems can also affect the family economically. It is difficult for adults with ADHD to be involved in financial matters or take care of their family finances. They often lose jobs, get fired frequently, and have trouble doing their jobs adequately because of their unpredictable behavior.

In order to avoid damaging their family, adults with ADHD need to learn how to control their behavior and mannerisms in order to be able to lead a normal and healthy life. Their families may also need assistance in dealing with their problems and understanding how they can help their loved one rather than complaining about the daily struggles of the adult with ADHD.

Effects on Society

An individual with ADHD has difficulty learning social skills, like how to get along with others, deal with feelings, express opinions, solve problems cohesively and communicate. This disability can cause the person to be isolated from society. Adults with ADHD may have trouble getting along with others because they are unable to understand others' feelings, perspectives and motivations. They also may not be able to see or understand the differences between their own behaviors and those of others. They may not even know how to express their feelings, and may not be aware of how their behavior affects others.

The behavior of those with ADHD can also lead to an increased risk of accidents that could cause harm to them or others around them. It has been reported that adults with ADHD are involved in more accidents than others, particularly on the road. This is because the symptoms of ADHD affect their driving skills. Adults with ADHD have a greater tendency to be involved in traffic accidents because of their impulsive behavior and short attention span. Moreover, they do not know how to properly react when encountering a dangerous situation on the road. It makes them more vulnerable to injury and death in car crashes.

ADHD has been found to have a negative impact on the economy due to the decrease in productivity and loss of working hours. Adults with ADHD are often unable to do their designated tasks. This results in them being absent from work, losing their jobs, and having trouble maintaining their job performance. The resulting decrease in productivity reduces the revenue of society as a whole, which can result in higher unemployment rates.

Adults with ADHD may also become involved in crime due to their inability to control their behaviors and anger. This lack of self-control makes it hard for them to stay out of trouble, especially when they get angry.

They also may take part in problematic behavior like alcoholism and eating disorders. They drink too much and take in large amounts of food to feel comfort and forget about their troubles. Both problems can lead to even more serious problems, like violence, smoking, and drug abuse.

CHAPTER 3: VARIOUS FORMS OF ADHD

These are different types of ADHD, all of which are characterized by impulsivity, hyperactivity, and/or inattention:

1. Predominantly Inattentive Type

This type is also referred to as "ADD" or Attention Deficit Disorder.

The child will have a difficult time paying attention and will often daydream, becoming distracted by other things going on around them. If they are able to focus their attention it is usually on something that interests them at the time. They will have a hard time following instructions that they do not find interesting or engaging, which could lead to them not completing assigned tasks. They will often play by themselves and when they do interact with others, they tend to lose track of the situation at hand. This can result to a lot of misunderstandings and hurt feelings.

The adult may also struggle in school, especially if they have difficulty paying attention in class. This is because their daydreaming makes school work appear boring. While they may have a hard time staying focused on important tasks, their attention can be easily diverted towards something that captivates them.

2. Predominantly Hyperactive Type

This is also referred to as "ADHD" or Attention Deficit Hyperactive Disorder. This is a form of hyperactivity where a person will have a very hard time staying in one place for an extended period of time. Their minds tend to wander, which leads them to not focus on what they are supposed to be doing. They will often act out in class, showing signs of hyperactivity by not sitting still or finishing their work. When they are doing a task that is dull or boring, they will have a hard time focusing on it and completing it. They will often have trouble staying interested in the things that other people find to be interesting. This type of ADHD can lead to issues with completing school work, not finishing tasks or assignments, daydreaming, and not being able to sit still when necessary.

3. Predominantly Impulsive Type

This type of ADHD can lead to risky behavior. The person will find themselves chasing something that they are interested in but their impulsivity will cause them to react without thinking about the consequences. They may even lie for no reason at all, which can lead to further problems. This type of ADHD can also lead to social problems, where they may have trouble staying friends with someone that they believe is boring or that doesn't agree with them on certain issues. The person may also be easily angered over small matters. They will often interrupt conversations, tend to blurt out comments at inappropriate times, and generally react impulsively and without thinking. They may even take unnecessary risks in order to prove something.

4. Predominantly Inattentive and Impulsive Type

This type of ADHD is a combination of two previously discussed types, which makes it very difficult to deal with. The person will have trouble focusing their attention on what they are supposed to be doing, and they will also be easily distracted by other things happening around them. They will often daydream, become absorbed in their own thoughts, and have a hard time following instructions. This does not mean that they cannot complete tasks but they may have trouble staying focused. Inattentional Inhibition is a theory where children with ADHD can focus their attention on a new environment but it will be almost impossible for them to focus their attention on what is going on in the present environment. This leads them to have a hard time finding balance between both of these things.

5. Predominantly Hyperactive and Impulsive Type

This type is the strongest of the three previously discussed types, which makes them very difficult to deal with. This person will have trouble focusing their attention, which can lead to them being easily distracted by something new happening in the environment. They will often react to things in an inappropriate way, causing them to act out. They will also find it very difficult to stay focused on their tasks. They may become bored and frustrated because they can't stay focused on their tasks. It is very important for children with this type of ADHD to make sure they get the proper amount of sleep and physical activity.

ADHD symptoms

The symptoms of ADHD can vary from person to person. Some adults may exhibit more symptoms than children, while others will exhibit the opposite. It is important to talk to a professional if you believe you or a loved one has ADHD. They will be able to diagnose the disorder and provide a treatment plan that everyone involved can follow.

Here we will discuss the symptoms of ADHD.

1. Inattention

The main symptom of ADHD is inattention. A person with inattention will find it difficult to pay attention to things that are going on around them and may find it impossible to concentrate on something for a long period of time. They will often feel like they cannot focus and will lose their train of thought when trying to concentrate on what they are doing at the moment. It can be very difficult for them to complete their work, come up with new ideas, remember things or follow instructions.

2. Hyperactivity

Hyperactivity is another symptom of ADHD. People with this symptom will find it hard to stay in one place for a long period of time and may even feel restless and overly full of energy. They may also have a hard time controlling their emotions and tend to be easily irritated, which can lead to outbursts and anger issues.

3. Impulsive

Impulsive behavior is something that often occurs with ADHD, causing the person to react without thinking about the possible consequences or how they will react when faced with them. They might act out inappropriately because they are excited about something, which can lead to problems with their behavior. They might also act without thinking at all.

4. Disorganization

Adults with ADHD tend to struggle in this area, which can cause problems for them at work or school. The proper organization of their tasks and assignments is normally difficult for them, although they can complete these tasks once they get started on them. They may also have a hard time remembering things such as work deadlines and other important dates.

5. Stress

This is a very common problem with adults with ADHD. They will often find themselves stressed or overloaded by their work or school, which can cause them to not complete projects on time or complete tasks that they should otherwise complete easily. They may also have a hard time recognizing when the stress in a situation is too high and they should seek help for their issues.

6. Inappropriate Fears

This is another very common problem with adults with ADHD. The slightest stress or an uncontrollable desire can cause them to have many inappropriate fears. They may be afraid of being lost or alone, but they will often worry about other things as well. These fears may lead to a lot of anxiety and being very scared all the time.

7. Sleeping Problems

This can include things such as oversleeping, late night disturbances, or staying up half the night to complete a work assignment. They may also have a hard time going to sleep when they need to because their thoughts are still going a mile a minute.

8. Boredom

This can occur when a person in a situation in which there are not enough things to do to keep them interested. Being bored is the biggest trigger of other ADHD symptoms.

9. Excessive Touching

This can include touching objects or people. It can also be part of a repetitive behavior in which they will touch the same thing over and over again. A person with ADHD may also touch themselves more than is standard, as a way of coping with their frustration.

10. Excessive Talking

This can include interrupting others, talking excessively without thinking about what they are saying or saying things that may be considered inappropriate. It can also be part of a repetitive behavior where they will talk for an extended period of time without getting any reaction from the people around them.

CHAPTER 4: FACTORS CONTRIBUTING TO ADHD

While there is no exact cause of ADHD, there are a number of things that have been linked to the disorder.

1. Genetics

While the exact gene that has been linked to ADHD has not been discovered, it is believed that there may be a genetic link to the disorder, which means it could be passed down generation after generation. While there are many genes that have been linked to ADHD, none of them have been confirmed as the cause of the disorder.

2. Brain chemistry

There have been a number of studies that have shown that the brain chemistry of people with ADHD is different from those without it. They tend to have lower levels of neurotransmitters such as dopamine, acetylcholine, and norepinephrine, all of which are important for the regulation of someone's behavior and attention span.

3. Environment

Another factor that has been found to play a role in the onset of ADHD is the environment. This includes the child's family life, including how they were raised, and their relationships with their parents. Additionally, it can include a child's school or their social life, including how often they spend time with others and whether or not they have a job.

4. Stress

There can be a number of different environmental factors that can cause ADHD in adults. These factors may include social pressure to act like an adult, and access to things like drugs, alcohol, and cigarettes. It also includes stress. This can play a large role in ADHD adults, who may find it difficult to cope with these factors.

5. Illness or disease

There are some diseases that have been linked to ADHD. Diabetes has been tied to the disorder, as well as Crohn's disease and some cases of lupus. It is unknown whether these links will prove to be definitive or not, but the chances of developing ADHD are greater for people who have one of these diseases.

6. Lack of sleep

Adolescents and adults with ADHD are more likely to be sleep deprived than those who do not have the disorder. It has been shown that children with ADHD are more likely to stay up later than their peers, which can affect their ability to concentrate, process information, and organize themselves for school or work. There has also been evidence that suggests sleeplessness can lead to lower levels of certain neurotransmitters in the brain.

7. Age

The likelihood of developing ADHD tends to increase as a person ages. While there is no exact number of years involved in this process, it is possible that the process occurs faster for those who have children with the disorder than those who do not.

8. Significant life events

There are some events that can lead to ADHD. Accidents, moving, or difficult family situations, are among the situations that are believed to trigger the onset of ADHD symptoms, or make them worse.

9. Psychological trauma

While there is no exact evidence to confirm this, it is possible that psychological trauma could lead to ADHD in adults. This trauma may be from a physical pain or a mental pain, such as a traumatic childhood experience. It can also include a loss of a close friend or family member. This can be a very traumatic time for most people, which makes it more likely that they will suffer from PTSD and other psychological disorders.

10. Drug abuse

Drug abuse can cause a number of different changes in the brain and body, which could be the cause of ADHD for some people. For children and teens, their brains are still developing and it is possible that small amounts of drugs such as marijuana could affect their ability to process information. This makes it more possible that they will receive a diagnosis of ADHD later in life.

11. Heavy metals

Heavy metal exposure has be linked to ADHD as well. While this has yet to be definitively proven, it is believed that exposure to heavy metals such as mercury could cause the disorder.

12. Genetically modified foods

While there is no evidence to show that genetically modified foods are specifically linked to ADHD, studies have shown that they are linked to other problems in the body including allergies and organ damage. This means it is possible that these foods could play a role in ADHD, especially for those who are sensitive to them.

13. Pesticides

There is also some evidence that pesticides could be linked to ADHD. This includes chemicals like pyrethrum, which can be harmful to people who are exposed to it. It may cause problems with their nervous system and reduce their ability to process information correctly.

14. Feeding patterns

There is some evidence that suggests that early childhood feeding times can lead to ADHD. This includes breastfeeding for a longer period of time, as well as giving a child an unlimited amount of food when they are young. Both of these have been linked to ADHD in children.

15. Environmental toxins

The environment is one of the major factors that can lead to ADHD in adults. These toxins can build up in a person's body and cause serious changes that can affect their ability to function in society or at school or work.

16. Prenatal Issues

Prenatal issues can also play a role in ADHD. This includes cases in which the mother smoked during pregnancy, or took alcohol or drugs. The child is more likely to have ADHD if either of these factors occured.

CHAPTER 5: IDENTIFYING ADHD: A GUIDE TO DIAGNOSIS

The diagnosis of ADHD is based on the history and results of a detailed head-to-toe physical examination, interviews with parents or guardians and teachers, and any previous psychological evaluations. All people with symptoms of ADHD should be thoroughly examined by a qualified screening professional before receiving an ADHD diagnosis.

There are several professional organizations that have published guidelines for the diagnosis of ADHD in children and adults.

Chemical testing

Although ADHD has been linked to a chemical imbalance in the brain, there is no simple way to test for this chemical imbalance. However, some healthcare professionals can order specific tests (blood and urine) to look for other problems such as thyroid disease, or other conditions that can cause symptoms similar to those of ADHD.

Cognitive testing for adults

Two types of cognitive testing may be done. One is an intelligence test, which looks at how well a person does on a set of tasks that test general knowledge, reasoning and creativity. This type of test will identify those with intellectual disabilities as well as those whose IQ is "borderline." The other type of cognitive test looks at memory, attention and executive function. This is the type used to diagnose ADHD.

Psychological tests

Psychological tests may be used to assess the severity of the symptoms of ADHD, how these symptoms affect an individual's ability to carry out activities at home, school or work, and how these affect mood and behavior.

The presence of ADHD will not automatically lead to school or work problems. However, ADHD can make it more difficult for an individual to focus on tasks without becoming distracted. This may impact reading comprehension. The brain fog associated with ADHD can also make concentration more difficult when reading or listening to others. People with ADHD may also have trouble following through on assignments or chores, or completing work in a timely manner due to their impulsiveness, forgetfulness and disorganization.

At school, people with ADHD might be labeled as lazy or unmotivated by teachers. At home, they may be criticized for being disorganized or having poor personal hygiene. These labels can reinforce the negative aspects of ADHD in any child or adult with the disorder. He may become depressed, anxious, or angry.

Psychologists test for ADHD by administering a number of different tests. If someone has already received a diagnosis of ADHD, the psychologist might give the person a standardized questionnaire to assess how severe his or her symptoms are.

Psychologists also use other types of tests to measure attention span, working memory, response time and impulsiveness. They also look at self-concept and self-esteem.

If the person's scores on these tests indicate that he or she may have ADHD, then additional testing is done, using interviews and questionnaires to assess the person's level of self-esteem, anxiety and depression.

During all psychological testing, psychologists look for other psychiatric disorders that may be causing the ADHD symptoms to occur. For example, someone who has ADHD with depression or anxiety may not be diagnosed with ADHD until these conditions are treated.

ADHD can cause problems in many areas of a person's life. The psychologist can determine if a person's symptoms are severe enough to warrant a diagnosis of the disorder. To make the diagnosis, a person must have at least six of nine specific inattentive or hyperactive/impulsive symptoms that have been present since childhood and continue through adulthood.

It is important to note that a diagnosis of ADHD does not mean that a person is "bad" or "lazy." The diagnosis only means that the other symptoms have been present for a long time and impair that individual's daily functioning. To receive an official diagnosis, people must have a number of symptoms in both categories. Because many children and adults with the disorder function well in certain areas of their lives and can hide or mask their symptoms, it may be difficult for them to get the proper treatment and learn strategies to help them be successful.

The psychologist will explain the results of the evaluation to the person being tested. This makes it much easier for all the people involved to understand what is causing these problems and how they can be treated.

The evaluation may also include information from the person's parents, teachers, or partner. These people can provide insight into how ADHD affects his or her everyday life.

Psychologists use diagnostic tools in their evaluations. The person being evaluated will have a chance to fill out a questionnaire or take a standardized test, which will indicate whether he or she has ADD/ADHD. The psychologist will use the results of this evaluation to help determine if ADHD qualifies as a true medical illness.

Psychologists also conduct psychological tests that evaluate the individual's cognitive functioning. These tests focus on how well the individual can think and learn, organize information and manage time and space. Psychological tests often include:

- Memory and attention capabilities (particularly focusing and staying on task)

- Ability to plan and use information

- Problem-solving and decision-making skills

- Understanding of social cues and behaviors

- Ability to control impulsive behavior (e.g. impatience, inappropriate activity level)

Psychologists might also ask the individual to keep a daily record of his or her behavior for a few weeks. This will help the psychologist evaluate how these behaviors affect everyday life. It helps give information about whether or not ADHD is causing problems in certain situations or with certain people. The psychologist may also talk with the individual's partner or parents to get their perspective on how he or she functions at home, at school and in other social settings.

After completing the evaluation and considering all relevant information, a psychologist can make a diagnosis and present his or her findings to the individual and his or her family members. The psychologist will then work with them to develop a treatment plan that can help that person lead a more fulfilling life.

Psychologists will evaluate their progress regularly and revise the treatment goals as needed.

Who is at risk of ADHD?

1. Children

ADHD is very common in children, and those who were born prematurely could be at a higher risk of the condition. This is because their brains might not have developed properly before they were born, which can cause problems with attention and other brain functions. Children aged 12 and younger may be at a higher risk of ADHD, especially if they have a family member who has been diagnosed.

2. Adults

Adults who have been diagnosed with ADHD in the past are more likely to get the disorder again when they get older. This is because their brain has not fully developed, which can cause it to diminish or get worse over time. It is possible that adults who have been diagnosed with depression may also suffer from ADHD, especially if they were depressed during their childhood.

3. Women

Some studies have shown that women are at a higher risk of ADHD than men. They tend to be more impulsive and out of control than men, which can lead to problems with focus and organization. Having a child is also considered to be a strong risk factor for ADHD in women, and it can cause many problems with their ability to care for their children and deal with anxiety.

4. The overweight/obese

Being overweight or obese can lead to a number of medical issues. These include high blood pressure, high cholesterol, and diabetes, which all have a link to ADHD.

5. Adolescents

Adolescents who are in their late teens and early twenties have a higher risk of ADHD because their brains are still maturing, which can lead to poor coordination and attention issues.

6. Women suffering from postpartum depression

This is a type of depression that usually develops after a woman gives birth. This can cause behavioral problems and poor focus because the brain has been changed drastically by childbirth. It can cause problems with concentration and attention, as well as poor coordination and organization skills.

7. Those living in poverty

While not everyone living in poverty will get ADHD, it is well known that children who grow up in low-income areas are more likely to develop the disorder. This is likely because of exposure to excessive alcohol, caffeine, and other chemicals that can affect their brains.

8. Those suffering from carcinogenic exposure

Exposure to carcinogenic compounds like lead paint may be linked to ADHD. This may cause damage to nerve and brain cells, which can lead to problems with attention and focus.

9. Smokers

There is evidence that smoking cigarettes during pregnancy can be linked to ADHD in newborns. Smoking can directly affect the development of an unborn baby's brain, which can lead to problems with attention and other skills.

Diagnostic Tests for ADHD

The following tests are provided in a brief diagnostic package for adults with ADHD. These tests will help you to qualify for a diagnosis of Attention Deficit Hyperactivity Disorder (ADHD). The clinician may then consult the more comprehensive and detailed criteria specific to your case.

Test #1: Self-Assessment Test

This questionnaire is designed to measure changes in your level of mental stimulation. It also examines your ability to concentrate for long periods of time and how easily distracted you get on a daily basis.

Test #2: The Think Aloud Test

This test is designed to see how well you can respond to simple questions and tests during the interview process. It gives the clinician a good idea of your ability to follow verbal and written instructions and cope with several tasks simultaneously. It also tests your short-term memory and auditory discrimination skills.

Test #3: Continuous Performance Test

This computerized test measures your ability to sustain your concentration over a specific period of time without distraction. When the test is complete, your performance will be evaluated and compared to patients with ADHD.

Test #4: Bender Gestalt Test

This test is designed to determine the extent of your cognitive impairment. It is used to identify how well you analyze, and your perceptual-motor skills. Visual perception, spatial relationships, form discrimination, and depth perception are among the things that are measured by this test.

Test #5: The Self-Report Form of the Toronto School Board Achievement Test (TS-BAT)

This test is designed to measure your level of emotional and social competence. It can help determine how you interact with others, your ability to express yourself, and your ability to cope with the problems and stresses of daily life. It also evaluates your academic and social skills.

Test #6: The Cooper-White Test

This test measures your level of motor coordination, attention, memory, speed of information processing, and reaction time. It is used to determine how well you can orient yourself in space and your capacity for planning ahead.

Test #7: The Time Crisis Test

This test measures how well you handle the stress of time pressures. It tests your ability to problem-solve under trying conditions. It is designed to help you focus on the tasks at hand without getting distracted by other tasks.

Test #8: The Stroop Test

This test measures your ability to inhibit inappropriate behavior when you are in an emotionally aroused state. It is believed that this test is able to detect behavioral problems in the areas of impulse control, self-regulation, and behavioral flexibility.

Test #9: The Frontal Lobe Evaluation Scale (FLES) Test

This questionnaire was developed by researchers in order to identify whether someone has a frontal lobe lesion. It examines your personality, your ability to cope with stressful situations, and your mental health over a period of time.

Test #10: The Bender Visual-Motor Gestalt Test

This test is made to detect the presence of a brain injury. It examines a person's capacity for visual perception and perceptual-motor abilities. This test is commonly used in clinical studies where there is a need to quantify any damage caused by brain injuries sustained during an accident or from exposure to head trauma.

Types of ADHD tests (ADHD scales)

The ADHD scales are designed to assess the level of ADHD symptoms. They are sometimes referred to as ADHD symptom scales.

The ADHD scales are designed to measure executive functioning abilities in adults with ADHD, however, they cannot detect all differences between adults with ADHD and adults without the disorder.

There are three types of scales that fall under this category:

1. Self-Assessment Rating Scales (SRRS)

These scales ask respondents questions about their personal experience of living with ADHD. There is no information given about other people's experiences or how others view them unless respondents explicitly say that they would like to know other peoples' perspectives on the topic. They are often the most accurate of the scales in terms of reflecting your true level of ADHD. However, people with more severe levels of ADHD may over-report their symptoms, which can also lead to an inflated score. This is why it is important to read the instructions closely.

2. Observed Rating Scales (ORS)

These are "objective" rating scales in that they are based on the observations of an outside observer. They are less likely to be influenced by the degree of motivation or ability to report symptoms than self-report scales. The rating scale should indicate who will complete the rating, how long it takes, and how the ratings should be completed. Ratings are often completed by the clinician or researcher. Observed rating scales do not assess cognitive aspects of ADHD, nor do they measure subjective experiences of daily functioning.

3. Direct Assessment Scales (DAS)

These scales are based on the direct assessment of ADHD symptoms by an experienced clinician or researcher. For this reason, they are frequently considered the "gold standard" for measuring ADHD symptoms. The scales should indicate how long it takes to complete them and where they should be completed (i.e. office). DAS's often include a series of questions about mental health, everyday activities, school performance, and occupational behavior. Some of the scales may ask about friends or family members that you interact with frequently. These scales can be quite long and will take considerable time to complete.

What is a differential diagnosis?

Differential diagnosis is the process of knowing which illness or condition may be causing observed symptoms. It involves comparing the possible diagnoses against one another and then narrowing it down to just one. This entire process can often take weeks, months, or even years to complete! Doctors will typically rule out the most common causes first before investigating more obscure conditions or illnesses that may also fit with observed symptoms. To make a differential diagnosis, the doctor will rule out certain causes of symptoms first. The remaining causes are then compared against one another and one is selected as the best match. Ideally, the cause should be both likely and correct. A proper differential diagnosis typically depends on the medical knowledge, experience, and skills of the diagnosing physician(s).

The most important part of determining a differential is to see if there are any medical conditions or illnesses that may be responsible for causing ADHD symptoms. The differential diagnosis involves two parts: the different diseases that may be causing the present illness, and common conditions that can also cause similar symptoms. Since there is no single test to diagnose ADHD, doctors must carefully consider all possible conditions. A doctor must consider the patient's age, sex, and demographic factors such as race and ethnicity in order to make an accurate diagnosis. Certain diseases and disorders such as diabetes, stomach ulcers, and lead poisoning can cause many of the same ADHD symptoms, such as hyperactivity and inattention. A physician is required to be certain that a disease or disorder exists before treating it. Treatment is optional with these conditions.

Another important part of the differential diagnosis is to consider any medications a person may have taken. There are several medications that have adverse side effects and can cause ADHD symptoms. These side effects can be mistaken for ADHD. When a person uses certain medications there is the potential for hyperactivity, inattention, and possibly even forgetfulness. A number of medications can be easily eliminated from consideration, while others may require a more comprehensive analysis before any detrimental side effects can be ruled out. A physician can help a person rule out specific medications as a causal factor in their current condition.

Treatment is not typically necessary with the primary differential diagnoses. With most primary conditions, treatment is aimed more towards symptom management than towards curing or eliminating the disease or disorder itself. The doctor will usually only treat ADHD symptoms if they are severe enough to affect daily functioning and if they will not be resolved through treatment of another medical problem.

How doctors make a diagnosis

Most doctors will use the following guidelines to make their differential diagnoses:

What's the cause? Doctors use an organized approach to make a differential diagnosis. In some cases, a visit with a behavioral therapist may reveal how the patient is reacting to different external factors. The behavioral therapist will interview and observe the patient during or after a stressful encounter. Behavioral therapists or psychiatrists may discover that specific life events have an impact on mood and overall behavior, while some patients report that certain foods affect ADHD symptoms.

What are the symptoms? After ruling out possible causes, another important step in making a differential diagnosis is looking at common symptoms that are present with the patient's condition. It is important for doctors to understand how these symptoms are explained by medical literature. Doctors will use a variety of reference materials, including published articles and research studies to determine if there are any other similar cases existing with the same observed symptoms. A physician may look at various medical journals to compare their case with others that have similar findings.

What is the treatment? Differential diagnosis is used to rule out possible diagnoses before proceeding with treatment. This can be especially important in cases where there are many different treatment options available. Doctors must first determine what specific disease or disorder exists before deciding how best to treat it. Doctors will always choose the treatment that is best for the patient if many different options are available. In some cases, a patient might not need any treatment at all. For example, ADHD is currently considered a behavioral disorder by medical science. While medication can benefit children with ADHD, it is not always necessary. If doctors determine that the cause of the problem is poor parenting skills, then they will try to rehabilitate these parents in order to fix the problem, rather than using drugs.

CHAPTER 6: ADDRESSING ADHD: APPROACHES TO TREATMENT

The right treatment is often the most important step in dealing with ADHD. Although treatment often provides immediate relief to symptoms, there are many potential complications that can occur. A thorough understanding of the condition and its treatment will help an individual deal with ADHD successfully.

What can I do at home?

The initial thing an individual should do when dealing with ADHD is to keep a journal. A journal will help you track your progress and track down any areas of improvement or relapse after treatment has begun. You can make it a goal to be more organized by practicing good time management. A good journal will help you determine how much time you are spending on different tasks each day. Keeping constant track of tasks will also help identify what is causing any sudden changes in behavior. You should also learn how to relax and take breaks. It is important to take breaks at least every hour or so during the day, especially if there are difficult tasks that require concentration.

How should I act around people?

The social skills of an individual dealing with ADHD will need to be modified when in social situations. For example, someone who has ADHD will need to be mindful of their behavior when in public places. They may not be able to pay attention to or remember small details in a conversation or in an environment, which may cause them to stand out negatively in the eyes of others. They may need to take a break from conversations or environments that will cause them to be distracted. Another strategy for social situations is to become more of a listener during conversations, rather than a talker.

How can I succeed in school?

If a person struggles in school, it may be because of their ADHD. Schoolwork and homework is often thought of as boring and painful, but it can also lead to very positive outcomes when dealing with ADHD in the future. ADHD symptoms often cause a person to lose focus on academic work and forget what they have learned. This can result in poor achievement in the classroom. A person with ADHD may also need to be very organized when it comes time to study for important exams. It is important for a person with ADHD to make sure that all work is completed on time because missing deadlines can cause them to lose marks or even fail an exam altogether.

What is the best way to deal with stress?

Stress can be a major contributing factor in causing ADHD symptoms to flare up. When an individual with ADHD is experiencing severe stress, their symptoms may increase. Stress also negatively affects personal relationships and work performance. When dealing with multiple problems at once, stress can cause people dealing with ADHD to become overwhelmed and frustrated. To deal with stress, it is really important to take care of yourself by eating healthy, staying active and getting enough sleep. Many people may also find that exercising can help alleviate their stress. This is because exercise increases blood flow to the brain, which helps reduce stress throughout the body.

Types of treatment

The kind of treatment your doctor recommends for your ADHD may be very different from the treatment you want or need. No one type of treatment fits everyone, and as such, there may be other options that could work better for you.

Medications are the most popular type of treatment. It's up to you to make a judgment whether this will work for you. ADHD medications can decrease the symptoms of ADHD and increase your ability to focus and concentrate. They can help you release more dopamine in the brain, which can help you feel less restless and develop more self-control.

Another treatment option is psychological or psychotherapy. Psychotherapy is the process of learning to treat your own mental health problems. Psychotherapists might tell a story to a person who has a hard time focusing, using all five senses, or by using guided imagery. Psychotherapy often involves a teacher and usually lasts several months to several years, although some forms include shorter therapy sessions, such as supervisory therapy and intensive therapy. Psychotherapy is used to treat many other types of mental health conditions, including depression, anxiety disorders, and personality disorders. Psychotherapy is often the first treatment given after medication has stopped working.

Psychotherapy can help you learn to cope with ADHD symptoms without medication. But psychotherapy does not cure ADHD; it can only help you become more comfortable with your brain's behavior. Psychotherapists are trained to help you develop adaptive coping strategies for your behavioral problems.

If psychotherapy is not the best option for you, consider trying other treatments such as cognitive-behavioral therapy (CBT) or EMDR therapy.

Cognitive-behavioral therapy (CBT) is a very effective method of treating ADHD, and it can help you reduce the use of medication. CBT often includes psych education about ADHD and how it affects your life, self-management strategies, and skills training for academic and social activities. But CBT does not teach you to control your behaviors; it only helps you learn how to manage them.

Both medication and psychotherapy can alleviate symptoms of ADHD, but they don't cure the disorder. If you've been treated and symptoms continue to cause problems, you may want to seek more help.

You may also consider counseling. If you choose to see a therapist, you'll want to find one with expertise in ADHD. You'll also want to find one who is willing to work with you on lifestyle issues, such as time management and organization.

And if it's not working, seek another one. And another one after that. Don't settle for treatment that isn't effective or that leaves you feeling worse than when you started.

Drug Therapy for Adult ADHD

Adderall is a brand of medication used to treat ADHD. It stimulates activity in the brain and improves concentration and focus.

Scientists believe that it works by helping the brain find its optimal state as it processes information. For people with ADHD, Adderall can lead to improved concentration, increased memory, and reduced impulsivity. It's also known as an "enhanced release" drug because it delivers medication into the brain over a much longer time than other kinds of stimulants (e.g., dextroamphetamine).

Adderall is a combination drug that includes both dextroamphetamine and amphetamine, which are stimulants. The amphetamine in Adderall stimulates brain chemicals called neurotransmitters that are responsible for feelings of motivation, wakefulness, pleasure, concentration, memory, and learning.

The benefit of using Adderall over other types of stimulants is that it has a longer "half-life" in the body. In other words, Adderall stays in the body for up to 12 hours after it's taken, whereas other drugs like Ritalin only last about four hours. This means that Adderall has a longer effect on the body and can be taken less frequently than other drugs.

Adderall is generally prescribed to treat adults with ADHD. It can also help people who are not diagnosed with ADHD but have symptoms like concentration problems or hyperactivity.

It's best for adults to take Adderall in the morning because it can sometimes cause insomnia. Adults should consult their physician before taking this drug because it can have some serious side effects, including an increase in blood pressure, heart rate, and body temperature.

Adults who take this drug should be aware that it can become addictive. It may also cause restlessness or insomnia if taken late at night.

For adults who don't like the way that Adderall makes them feel, there are several other types of medication for ADHD. One type of stimulant works by blocking the body's production of dopamine – this is why some people experience feelings of euphoria when taking these medications.

There are several other types of drugs that are used to treat ADHD. Doctors can prescribe antidepressants, beta blockers, and anti-anxiety medications to help patients manage the symptoms of ADHD.

Antidepressants are often used to treat depression or anxiety disorders in adults with ADHD. It's been shown, however, that some people experience a worsening of symptoms while taking antidepressants. This is because they can make symptoms worse by disrupting normal brain chemistry and increasing anxiety.

Beta-blockers are used for treatment of high blood pressure, chest pain, irregular heartbeat, and tremors. These drugs can also be used to help people with ADHD who have co-occurring conditions like anxiety disorders.

Anti-anxiety medications are used to treat symptoms associated with ADHD that are related to stress or anxiety, for example, panic attacks or obsessive compulsive disorder. These medications can help with depression or anxiety, but they may also cause mild-to-moderate side effects.

In some cases, ADHD medications have been shown to be helpful for treating co-occurring disorders like anxiety and depression. In other cases, the drugs have been shown to worsen symptoms of anxiety and depression by disrupting brain chemistry. Since these drugs have a significant effect on the brain's chemistry, it's important that adults with ADHD consult a doctor before taking any type of medication.

The Role of the Psychologist

Psychologists can provide training and counseling. They can also help people with ADHD become more productive at school, work and home. This includes learning skills that will improve their ability to pay attention and focus on the tasks they need to complete. This may include strategies that involve time management skills such as organizing and prioritizing tasks.

Psychologists can also help people with ADHD improve their relationships with family, friends and co-workers. This may be accomplished by teaching them new ways to communicate with others. Parents of children with ADHD can learn how to help their child get his or her schoolwork done on time, get organized for school, and stay focused during the day.

Psychologists have also developed programs that teach social skills. Many people with ADHD have problems making friends because they are self-centered, impulsive or lacking in social skills.

CHAPTER 7: ADHD MANAGEMENT THROUGH BEHAVIORAL THERAPY

Though the core symptoms of ADHD typically improve with age, adults with ADHD can still benefit from behavioral therapy. Behavioral therapy can increase self-awareness and help people learn to control their inattention and hyperactivity.

Contingency management techniques can help adults who find it difficult to manage their behavior through punishment and reward. Although these methods don't work for everyone, they can be helpful in some cases and should not be overlooked as a treatment option.

Although many people with ADHD think of themselves as failures, this is simply untrue. Millions of people with ADHD are law-abiding, successful adults who have learned to control their disorder.

However, it is so important to remember that many people with ADHD seek treatment because they want to improve their lives, not because they need to be "fixed." Because of this belief, the need for support groups can sometimes feel unwelcome or threatening. This is why it is vital that you find the right one for you.

How Does Behavioral Therapy Work?

Behavioral therapy for ADHD uses the principles of learning theory to change behavior. The "learning" in behavioral therapy is usually carried out through modeling, coaching and feedback.

As an example, if you are having problems with time management, you can use a stop watch to time how long it takes for you to complete specific tasks. This way, if something isn't working right, then you can try to figure out why and determine what it would take to fix the problem.

Next, you can write down the key points that you could improve on and then create a plan to work on each relevant problem, over time.

Modeling means that the person with ADHD will observe how other people perform tasks. For example, someone might watch an expert juggler practice his juggling for 30 minutes and then try it out in front of their boss or classmates.

Coaching involves asking someone what they are thinking, feeling or doing during specific situations to learn how they can improve their behavior.

Finally, feedback can involve using questions to help people learn what they are doing right or wrong.

Because ADHD is a social problem, it is also important for people with ADHD to practice their new behaviors in stressful situations.

CBT for Adults

Cognitive behavioral therapy or CBT is primarily a talking therapy, and it is done over the short-term to bring a change in the way people think and instill healthy thought patterns. CBT for adults with ADHD is used to explore the thoughts and beliefs that cause problems for a person. Cognitive restructuring is a central component of CBT, and it involves challenging negative thought patterns.

The main idea behind CBT is to bring a change in how the person perceives the events of their lives. It also deals with how they behave in such situations. What CBT does is help the person with ADHD control their impulses by putting some space between the stimuli and responses.

CBT is shown to be effective for the treatment of adults with ADHD. A recent study found that it improved attention, behavior and social skills in adults with ADHD.

The main principles of CBT are as follows:

1. The person should be made aware of their emotions or feelings and any other reactions which might take place in their surroundings. The emotional indicator should be identified so that it can act as a precursor, giving an adult time to respond appropriately.

2. Improving the adult's ability to focus will let them identify the mistakes they are making in terms of time management, organization, etc., and accordingly take steps to rectify it.

3. The adult should be given the opportunity to recognize the warning signs that indicate their behavior is out of control.

4. The adult will also be trained to recognize specific areas where their disorder manifests itself. When problem areas are identified, it will then be possible for them to find ways to change them.

5. Another important principle of cognitive behavioral therapy for ADHD is that people are given tools to rectify problems, and provided with effective strategies for coping with their disorder.

A support group is another powerful tool that can be used to help with ADHD. A support group is a very effective way to identify problems and ask for help from others who have had the same experience.

How CBT Works

CBT is a process of addressing different avenues of a person's life in order to make positive changes. Adults with ADHD are taught what they need to learn in order to change their behavior and personality.

CBT may also involve the person with ADHD taking part in various exercises. These exercises can help them understand their thoughts better. They are also taught on how to control these thoughts.

CBT helps in correcting the following patterns:

1. All-or-nothing thinking

This type of thinking pattern is when a person consistently uses words like ever or never (i.e., absolute words). This is the kind of thinking that can make a person feel as if there is no chance for improvement.

2. Overgeneralizing

This refers to the tendency to view an event as having more negative implications that it actually has. For example, someone with ADHD may have a strong opinion about something. They will think, "I dread this event because I know I will mess up." This will lead them to believe that whatever they do, they will always fail.

3. Mental filtering

This kind of thinking happens when a person chooses to focus on just one negative detail instead of looking at the whole picture. An adult with ADHD can be too sensitive to negative words said by others. He will only remember the bad things that were said about him, and will ignore all the positive aspects.

4. *Jumping to conclusions*

This is when a person assumes that something bad might happen, even if there is no evidence for it. For example, if a person with ADHD was late for an appointment once, they would assume that they will be late again.

5. *Magnification*

This is when something is perceived as being worse than it really is.

6. *Emotional reasoning*

This happens when a person uses their feelings as a basis for proving something or justifying a certain action. If they feel that something is bad, then it must be so, even if there is no proof.

7. *Personalization*

This is when a person thinks that whatever is happening to them is somehow their fault. For example, if they were late and could not find a parking space, then they will assume it's because of their lateness and/or poor parking skills.

8. *"Should" statements*

This refers to using words like "must," "should" and "ought" as descriptors for judging someone else or oneself. For example, people with ADHD use the word "should" as in "I should be able to do this because I am smart. If you don't like it, then you should not give me any comments."

9. *Mind reading*

This is when someone assumes that the actions of another person are directly related to them. For example, if they witnessed another person's actions, they may assume it is because of some sort of injury or weakness on the part of the other individual.

10. Catastrophizing

This refers to assuming that something disastrous will happen whenever some sort of challenging situation arises. For example, an adult with ADHD may think that a particular project they are working on will end up being a miserable failure.

11. Labeling

This is when a person attaches a negative label to themselves. For example, when a person feels overwhelmed by their thoughts and emotions, they will be too sensitive about it and will think, "I am such a fool."

12. Emotional reasoning

This is when people assume that the actions of another person are directly related to them. For example, if they witnessed another person's actions, they may assume it is because of some sort of injury or weakness on the part of the other individual.

Strengthening Your Cognitive Skills

With these skills, you will gradually become more organized and less forgetful. You'll feel calmer, less frustrated, more patient, and will have an easier time managing your anger. These skills will enable you to complete your tasks more competently and with less stress. Make a commitment to yourself to learn these skills, even if you have to tackle only some of them at a time. Each skill will help you in some way, and they all contribute to a calmer, less distracted mind.

The eight cognitive skills are:

1. Visualization/Imagery

This skill involves visualizing or picturing in your mind the way you want something to be. It is particularly useful when trying to de-stress (for example, relaxing an angry face), which can help relax your muscles and produce better results in your work.

2. Metacognition

This skill involves evaluating your own thoughts and feelings. It helps you stay focused on what really matters in a situation so you will be able to control your thoughts and emotions instead of being controlled by them.

3. Self-monitoring

This skill involves taking good care of yourself so you maintain an optimal state of health and productivity at work and home. As with most skills, the more you use it, the more proficient you become at it. You can practice self-monitoring by using good time management techniques to manage your time, set work expectations that are realistic, and identify your strengths rather than your weaknesses.

5. Planning/Prioritizing

This skill involves preparing in advance for the future and organizing your thoughts into a logical sequence. Knowing when to expect things, knowing what is important and when, and knowing when to say no is all part of this skill. Using calendar software makes planning easier, but you can also plan by writing a to-do list with a priority system so you know what you must do first, second, etc., so that you have more time for the essential things.

6. Working Memory

This skill involves recalling information you've heard, read, seen, or experienced. It is also involved in learning new skills. It enables you to focus on doing one task at a time and not being distracted by other things vying for your attention.

7. Planning/Implementation

This skill includes the ability to organize things into action steps that will eventually lead to desired results. Your plans are expressed as goals for your work or home life involving daily tasks that include time estimates.

8. Processing Speed

This skill involves processing things quickly so you can complete tasks accurately and efficiently. This will allow you to save time and energy, but be careful not to cut corners so your work becomes compromised.

Each of these skills is essential if you want to improve the quality of your work, your effectiveness, and your level of satisfaction with yourself. By gradually working on each of these skills, you will become more organized and less frustrated.

CHAPTER 8: BOOSTING MEMORY ABILITIES FOR PEOPLE WITH ADHD

Many people who suffer from ADHD also suffer from memory problems. Luckily, there are a number of steps that can be taken to improve memory.

1. Diet

Having a diet rich in vitamins and minerals will help improve your memory by nourishing the brain. These vitamins include B12, B6, folic acid, and zinc. Saturated fats should be cut out of your diet to prevent damage to the nervous system, which can make it much harder for you to focus.

2. Exercise

Since many people with ADHD have issues with focus and memory, it is essential to exercise regularly. This will help the brain work harder and use more energy, which can promote the ability to process information.

3. Sleep

We all need sleep to function normally, but for those with ADHD, it's doubly important that they get a good night's sleep. This is because the brain needs to be able to rest in order for the mind to relax and revive itself. People who don't get proper sleep may have memory problems because the brain isn't able to heal and rejuvinate.

4. Medication

As discussed earlier, it can be a good idea for those with ADHD to take medication, especially if they suffer from a more severe form of the disorder. When taking medication, there are certain things doctors look out for in order to make sure you are not becoming dependent on them. For instance, it is not advised that people take medication containing amphetamines, since this may cause addiction to the drug. In most cases, stimulant medications are the best way to treat the disorder. These work by raising levels of dopamine in your brain, which causes movement in different parts of your mind.

5. Training

It's also important to condition your brain through training. This can be accomplished by doing puzzles, reading books, or playing games on a computer or mobile device to practice your focus and memory skills. All of these can train your brain to work harder and more efficiently, which can help you learn new things more easily.

6. Mindfulness

While mindfulness was not originally designed to work with ADHD, it can be very helpful for those who suffer from the disorder. Mindfulness is a mental state that is achieved through training the brain to focus on present activities and to pay attention to what is happening around you. It doesn't require you to do anything other than concentrate on your current thoughts, and can help those with ADHD focus on what they are doing without getting distracted by other things.

7. Relaxation

Relaxation techniques can also help those with ADHD. Techniques include deep breathing or light meditation. These can help you slow down your thoughts so you aren't constantly bombarded with them and can allow your brain to relax and heal itself.

8. Focus

Finding a way to focus on one thing at a time is important for those suffering from the disorder. A good way to concentrate on one thing is through using a timer. If you need to complete something, set a time in which to do it and then try to get all of the information required before that time is up. This will help reduce distractions and make sure you are able to focus more efficiently.

9. Technology

Technology can be a great tool in not only preventing distraction, but also helping your brain to work better. There are many different apps that can help stimulate the brain to pay attention better and focus more. Using them regularly will help you get rid of bad habits and learn how to focus properly.

Ways to Improve Focus

It's really hard to manage ADHD when you can't pay attention. But there are so many things you can to do to make things a little easier.

Give yourself simple, clear directions.

Verbal directions are best, but written or visual guides can also help. When possible, reduce the number of tasks you have to do in a single day by choosing activities that do not depend on other activities being done first.

Limit distractions.

Try to change your environment so that it is difficult for you to get distracted by other people or activities. Avoid using your computer in an area where you are exposed to frequent phone calls or interruptions. If you tend to get distracted by mail, for instance, don't leave it near your computer. Make it a habit of putting it in a different place every day. To help yourself stay focused, set rules for yourself when working at home or in the office.

Change your environment.

If you work in an area with poor lighting, move to a brighter environment. If noise is distracting, move to a more quiet place. Assign yourself one or two "to-do" tasks that you will complete when you get up in the morning, every afternoon during the day, and at night before bed.

Put yourself on a schedule.

Make a list of activities you need to complete, then follow this schedule throughout your day, even if it feels like overriding your ADHD is the only way you'll get tasks done. Find creative ways to stay focused. For example, listen to music with headphones when you are working on boring tasks that require attention for long periods of time. Put some sticky notes on your monitor or in your book when you need to concentrate on a task. Be sure to use a variety of ways to stay focused. Don't rely on just one approach.

Prepare for distractions.

When you have a job that involves a lot of paperwork, schedule active phone calls or meetings in your schedule so you don't have long periods where you are stuck with a lot of reading and writing to do. Avoid multitasking if it interferes with your ability to follow directions.

Take a break.

If your mind strays to something else or lots of "what if" thoughts pop up, try taking a break. Have a short walk around the block or around your office. Put your hands over your eyes and breathe deeply (for about three minutes). Do some stretching exercises (for about two minutes) or 10 sit-ups.

Play a game that requires concentration.

This can help you focus more intensely on a task with fewer distractions. Choose an activity from each of the following three categories:

- Physical

– Go outside and play a sport.

– Go for a walk.

- Mental

– Do mental math or recall with your eyes closed.

- Social

– Talk to someone you like or make conversation with someone whose company you enjoy.

– Paint, draw, or do some sort of craft.

Focus Plan:

Step 1: Write your goals for the day

1...____

2...____

3...____

4...____

Step 2: Identify triggers for your ADHD

1...____

2...____

3...____

4...____

Step 3: Identify what you will do when confronted with the trigger

1...____

2...____

3...____

4...____

Step 4: Identify a reward for sticking to the plan

1...____

2...____

3...____

4...____

Step 5: Identify something to do that will help you feel good about yourself today

1...____

2...____

3...____

4...____

Step 6: Identify a distraction or a reward you can do when you feel overwhelmed

1...____

2...____

3...____

4...____

Step 7: Reward yourself for sticking to the plan as well as the reward that you identified for yourself today

Step 8: Identify how you can do this again tomorrow.

1...____

2...____

3...____

4...____

Step 9: Fill in the blanks with what you accomplished today and praise yourself for sticking to your plan of action.

1...____

2...____

3...____

4...____

Ways to Manage Behavior

It can be hard to be mindful of your ADHD when you've got distractions all around you. But you don't have to do it on your own. Here are some things you can do to manage your behavior.

1. Work on helping yourself deal with distractions. Sometimes, there's nothing you can do about distractions that pop up, but taking steps to reduce their impact will help you feel more in control. If possible, go for a short walk or skip the computer entirely when you need to focus.

2. Keep a list of triggers. Use this to keep your mind from straying to other things when you need to focus.

3. Don't allow yourself to get bored. If the task is boring, change it up so you continue to feel productive and engaged.

4. Be sure not to become frustrated or angry at yourself for having ADHD, no matter how difficult it might be.

5. Always remember that you can feel better. The more you work on dealing with ADHD, the more you can learn to keep distractions from becoming overwhelming.

6. Ignore any people who say that ADHD doesn't exist, or that it is just an excuse for being lazy or rude. These are not the right people to hang out with, and they are probably just frustrated by their own inability to focus on the tasks at hand.

7. Set things up for success. If you're going to work on a task that requires a lot of focus, do everything possible to reduce the chances of getting distracted. For example, get rid of anything that makes noise in your immediate area, turn off e-mail notifications, and make sure your phone is on silent before you begin working.

8. Create a distraction-free zone. If you're going to use a computer, make sure that it's in a quiet area where there is no chance of being bombarded by visual or auditory distractions.

9. Remember that managing ADHD is not about what you can't do, but what you can do...even when it means doing things differently from other people with ADHD. Remember, different approaches will work for different people.

10. Make time for everything you like to do without feeling guilty. You can still have lots of fun in life. You just have to be willing to do things differently to people who don't have ADHD.

11. Keep your goals in mind at all times. This will help you remember what you're working toward, and will make it easier to put up with the obstacles along the way.

12. Remember that there is no generic solution for managing ADHD. Each person is different from the next, so it's important to be aware of the specific types of problems you have so you can help yourself, as well as those around you.

13. Don't let your ADHD control your life. Know that you can participate in social events, meet deadlines and complete assignments on time.

14. Remember that there are certain things you can't do anything about. Understand the things you can and can't change in life. Don't let yourself get overwhelmed by things outside of your control. There are times when it is necessary to put up with irritating distractions, which can make life even more challenging for those of us with ADHD. But at the same time, you do not have to let these things beat you down or make your life miserable.

15. If you find yourself getting distracted, slow down and focus on one thing at a time until you're finished with everything you need to do. If you still find yourself

distracted, consider how important the task at hand really is to you and whether or not there is a better time to do it.

16. Although many people with ADHD are disorganized, don't allow your work-place to become messy or chaotic.

17. Consider keeping a "to-do" list. This will help you remember the things you have to do not only today but also tomorrow and on future assignments. If you are having a hard time completing things on your to-do list, break each task down into a list of smaller tasks.

18. Remember that there is no reason to deny yourself the right to be who you are just because you have ADHD. You can accomplish your life's goals and still be true to yourself. There is no reason for you to give up on your dreams just because you're not like other people.

19. Positive thinking will help you control your thoughts, feelings, and actions and will make it possible for you to follow through on important tasks when faced with distractions or tempting diversions. Learn to view challenges in a positive way.

20. It's okay to say "I don't know." It is better to admit what you don't know than to pretend to know something you don't in order to avoid appearing foolish in front of others. It's okay to not be perfect, and it's okay to admit that you don't know something.

21. Don't forget to praise your achievements. This will help you to maintain a positive attitude and a sense of accomplishment, which will inspire you to continue working toward your goals.

22. Don't let yourself be overwhelmed by the effects of ADHD. It's possible for you to manage your emotions in a more compassionate way.

23. Never give up, even if others may be discouraging you from chasing your dreams. Don't let others set you up for a failure.

Steps to Manage your Behavior:

Step 1: Identify what is triggering your behavior.

1...____

2...____

3...____

Step 2: Identify what you are doing about the trigger and what you can do differently in future.

1...____

2...____

3...____

Step 3: What is something you can do that will help you feel good about yourself today?

1...____

2...____

3...____

Step 4: Identify a reward for sticking to your plan.

1...____

2...____

3...____

Step 5: Identify what you will do if this problem behavior persists or if it occurs again in the future.

1...____

2...____

3...____

Step 6: Identify what you will do when you feel upset with someone who is not supportive of you and your goals and dreams for yourself.

1...____

2...____

3...____

Managing your behavior may seem difficult at times. If you feel discouraged, depressed, or frustrated with yourself, think about all of the great things that you have accomplished this year and how far you have come.

Getting Organized

It can be very difficult to stay organized when you have ADHD, and it's easy to lose track of important items and tasks. Fortunately, there are many tools and techniques that can make life less stressful and more successful for those with the disorder.

Creating a Well-Organized Home

Although ADHD makes it difficult to stay organized, a big part of the problem could be a disorganized home. Clutter attracts clutter, and your job will be much easier if you begin with a clean, clutter-free space. Start by getting rid of things that don't bring you comfort or joy. Then, look for items that serve as distractions, such as toys and knickknacks, and donate them to charity.

Use Your Computer as an Organizer

Many individuals with ADHD love technology, and it can provide a great way to stay organized. Use your computer as a starting point for organizing, and begin by creating a filing system that will allow you to save and search for items quickly. For example, create folders based on topics – such as bills, ongoing expenses and school work – and then label them clearly so the information is easy to find and access.

Use a Planner

One of the biggest challenges for those with ADHD is remembering daily tasks and appointments. A planner is a great way to keep track of what you need to do, and it's also a tool you can utilize on a daily basis. Using a planner is simple – all you have to do is list what you need to do each day, and then cross off each task as it's completed. You can even set reminders in your schedule for important events or tasks that have due dates. The plan must be flexible, so modify it as needed and always be sure to do your work. . If you have trouble remembering appointments, carry around a pocket calendar with you. Use a desk diary or wall calendar for more detailed information.

Sorting your Mail

Some people with ADHD have difficulty regulating the flow of incoming messages into the mailbox and sorting out what needs attention and what is irrelevant or unnecessary. One such person I know organizes her mail into separate colored file folders to avoid losing track.

Sorting Your Desk/Desk Drawer

In a similar vein, use a sorting system for the contents of your desk. Use a color-coded file folder, and sort the contents within it by category: work-related papers, notes, meeting documents and so on. The same goes for your desk drawer. Use file folders to sort your papers and supplies by category.

Using Dividers to Organize Files or Notebooks

Dividers can be very helpful in organizing large files, notebooks or binders. They are especially useful if there are several people working on the same project or who need to access the same information at different times. You can also use dividers to keep individual things separate. For instance, you could have a file cabinet for important papers, a filing cabinet for your personal papers, and have another file drawer for smaller paperwork. You could also use dividers to keep separate projects separate. For example, you could have three different-colored folders for separate projects; then, if one project is finished, you can take it out of its file drawer and put it in the filing cabinet for the next project. If you're not sure how to use them, look through some of your papers or files and see what works best for you.

Using an Organizer

An organizer can come in handy when you have papers scattered around the house and need to quickly find information. If you've never used one before, it's probably best to start with an index card file or a notebook with pages in which you write down important dates or information that needs immediate attention. Index card files can also be useful for storing recipes, notes and shopping lists that you might not need on a regular basis, yet want to keep. An organizer is particularly helpful if you have difficulty holding on to paperwork.

Managing your Emotions

Your emotions are an important part of life. If you were not able to experience joy, sadness, anger, fear, frustration, loneliness, compassion or love, you would not be the same person. When you have ADHD, these emotions are sometimes stronger than they are for others because it is harder for someone who has ADHD to manage his/her emotions. Managing the intensity of your emotions involves controlling your physical responses to them so you can still remain focused on your task.

When your emotions are in control, you can plan for what to do in different situations rather than being controlled by your emotions. It is necessary to learn how to identify the intensity of an emotion so that you can respond accordingly. For example, if you feel angry because someone interrupted you and it is interfering with the quality of your work, then take a break for a few minutes and return to the task once you have calmed down.

If you are finding it hard to manage your emotions, try the following techniques:

1. Identify the emotion(s) you are feeling so that you can respond to it effectively.

2. Put the emotion into words. Say, "I feel frustrated."

3. Make an external goal that will help you control the emotion. One good example is to count backwards from five to one until your anger subsides. Another example might be to take a walk around the block or do push-ups or planks or other physical activity to release your anger before returning to the situation at hand.

4. Use positive self-talk that will help you cope with the situation. For example, "I can stay calm and in control."

5. If you keep having the strong emotion, leave the situation and return when you are in a much better state to deal with it.

6. Practice these techniques with different situations until they become second nature for you.

7. Be aware of your thoughts and feelings, and avoid dwelling on negative ones or feeling guilty about mistakes in the past. This will only make things worse.

8. Put things into perspective. Sometimes our emotions are stronger than they need to be based on the situation at hand. For example, if you are frustrated by an hour-long traffic jam, remind yourself that this is not a life-or-death situation.

9. Remember that you are responsible for your own emotions, and are not responsible for the actions of others unless they directly affect you.

10. Remember that you can change your emotional reactions by changing your thoughts. For example, if you convince yourself that the traffic jam is not that bad, then you will probably see it from a less angry perspective.

11. Remind yourself of positive things. Focus on all the good things that are happening in life and remind yourself of them to relieve some of your stress or anger.

12. If you feel powerless, remind yourself that the only thing you can control is your response to your feelings, and you can choose how to respond.

13. Recognize and point out the humor in some situations even if they are frustrating. This will help you and others around you feel better.

14. Express yourself with words or physical activity rather than holding everything in because it will impact your health negatively.

15. Use your imagination to help you cope with difficult situations. For example, imagine yourself as a superhero who is able to fly through the air or change into a fire-fighting firebird or even into a shark that can defeat the enemy. This will help you gain perspective on things that are not important and will allow you to regain control so that you can deal with what is important in your life and work effectively.

16. Read something motivational to keep you in a good mood. Sometimes if you are feeling frustrated it is because your emotions are low, and you can boost them by reading something that makes you feel better.

18. Breathe (take deep breaths) when you feel like you might be losing control or when your emotions seem too high.

19. Try meditation or yoga to help you deal with stress, anger, frustration, conflicts with others, etc.

CHAPTER 9: CONQUERING YOUR WEAKNESSES

Don't let your weaknesses dictate your life. ADHD should not prevent you from living a happy and successful life. It can even be used as an asset to help you overcome the challenges and problems you encounter in everyday life and in your career. You can use it to promote your independence and self-reliance in ways that will make you more enjoyable to be around. You can use it to help you rise above the negative influences that may be affecting your day-to-day life.

It's never too late to begin making something of your ADHD. At any age, you can set aside any negative feelings about how it has affected you in the past and begin working toward overcoming its challenges. Even if you have been struggling with something all of your life, it's never too late to get help from a counselor or psychiatrist who can help you work through your issues, develop coping skills, and find ways to use your ADHD in a way that benefits you more than it harms you. Starting today, you can create a new lifestyle for yourself that will allow you to overcome the misconceptions about ADHD.

Don't let anyone tell you that this is "impossible." No matter your age, you can find ways to overcome the problems of ADHD that are unique to you. You can begin today.

While this book provides you with some helpful information about ADHD, it does not replace the services of a trained professional who can help you reach your full potential. Always be sure to seek the advice of a professional before making major changes in your life, behavior or personality because there may be significant risks involved.

It's never too late to start working on overcoming your shortcomings with ADHD. Despite what you may have previously believed, you can begin working toward being the person you have always wanted to be. You can continue on your path of achieving your goals and setting new ones for yourself. Now that you've learned more about ADHD, it's time to start using what you have learned in order to overcome the obstacles that may be preventing you from being the person that you know yourself to be.

Starting Your Day Right

People with ADHD tend to struggle in the morning. This can make it difficult to get out of bed, get to work on time, and be productive. It is very important for adults with ADHD to make starting their day right a priority.

You can control your moods and attitude by changing the way you start your day. This is one of the most important chapters in this workbook – the early morning hours are crucial for your success, both at school and at work. Because your brain takes time to reach peak activity, getting up earlier gives you a better chance to be focused during the window of time when you are most productive. As you start your morning routine, take a few moments to consider what is important to you today. What is the single most important thing that you want to accomplish? This will provide motivation and direction. The key to motivating yourself in the morning is planning ahead.

A good morning routine will keep your brain alert and focused, which can help avoid some of the mistakes that people with ADD are prone to make. Planning when and where you will have breakfast, for example, will help reduce uncertainty about what you are going to do next. After waking up, refrain from going straight to your electronic devices. You don't have to check social media...so don't do it. Don't feel obligated to respond to every email or text message immediately.

As part of your morning routine is complete, consider getting up and going straight for a cold shower. This will wake your body up and your mind will be more alert. Now is the time for "center of attention" exercises, which are designed to help you focus, overcome distractions, and become more productive. Take the opportunity after the shower to jot down your goals for that day or transfer them into a digital recording device or keep them in a notebook. Plan what you are going to do during the day, including small, immediate tasks that must be done that morning. Your brain is more apt to work on these tasks when it is fresh and ready to go. Get these jobs done early so they are out of the way. This process will have a huge impact on your success during the rest of the day.

How to Stop Procrastination

Procrastination is a behavior that causes people to put off things they know they should do now. It means postponing important tasks tasks to a later time. We procrastinate by doing less important tasks, often because they are more comfortable.

People who procrastinate usually have poor time management skills and tend to be late for appointments. Procrastinators tend to rush their work, which leads to careless mistakes or imperfect tasks or projects. Furthermore, procrastination leads to poor productivity.

Procrastination can occur because we have bad habits such as losing track of time, feeling nervous, feeling tense and afraid, having little patience and lack of self-control. This behavior is mostly due to the feeling of not being in control. Procrastination can also occur due to thinking that we are better off doing something less important rather than dealing with the stressful tasks at hand. When we are procrastinating, we are holding back on our responsibilities.

The reason behind procrastination is usually that we want to escape the pressure and chaos of our necessary tasks. When we avoid doing what we need to do because we don't like the task or we are not prepared for it, it is a form of procrastination. The worst consequence of this behavior is that it leads people to feel stressed and exhausted when they finally do begin their work.

Procrastination is also linked to disorganization and difficulty staying focused when there is so much to do. Individuals with ADHD often struggle with these issues, which leads them to avoid tasks and wait until the last second before tackling them. This can result in the individual not completing their work to the best of their ability. This can lead to feelings of guilt and shame. They may feel like a failure and become upset.

Fear of failure is another reason why people procrastinate. When they start on a task or project, they realize it is more difficult than they thought it would be. This can make them feel hesitant and they start looking for an easier solution. This may lead them to fail at the task or project.

The first step is admitting you have a problem and stating your intention to change a habit. Write down in detail the obstacles in your way and the negative feelings associated with not doing what needs to be done.

Make a list of tasks or projects that you have been putting off doing and create an action plan on how you are going to attack those tasks. Be sure to have a specific deadline for doing them. It can be helpful if you write it down on a calendar or on a small notepad that you can keep handy. Then, break the task into small steps and complete each step as it is due.

Ask for help from a friend or family member if you are struggling with overcoming procrastination. Explain to them how it is affecting your relationships and your responsibilities. They should be willing to help you out by assisting in completing the task or project.

Make a change in the environment where you are going to work on the task or project. For example, if you are procrastinating about writing a report on your computer, try writing it on paper instead.

Another step is to make sure that you are not getting distracted. Organize your work by breaking the project or task into small steps and making sure you do each one before moving onto the next. This will be very helpful to make sure that you are not procrastinating.

You should also learn to look forward to doing the work. This will increase your motivation and help you stay focused on the task. Working with a therapist is another good way to help you overcome procrastination. He or she will help you find the cause of your procrastination and figure out a way to cope with it effectively.

Some people have a hard time managing their time well. To avoid procrastinating, try making daily schedules and stick to them as much as possible. If you find it difficult to stick to this routine, try using a planner or a diary to jot down your upcoming deadlines and tasks.

Procrastination can cause stress, anxiety and frustration, made worse by feelings of guilt. It is important to learn to stop procrastinating so you can enjoy life more and not feel as much stress. Once you understand what causes you to procrastinate you can learn how to stop doing so for good!

What to Do When Your Day Feels Rushed

We all have days where we feel totally overwhelmed. We run around trying to get so many things done within a short amount of time, leading us to feel stressed, upset, and frazzled.

If you have ADHD, you know that feeling well. You can be doing one thing and then you realize that there is something else that needs to be done before you can continue with your original task. Your mind is racing, and you find yourself jumping from one thing to another to the next. This makes it feel like your whole day is churned up.

There are a few things that will help you out. This section will cover some practical ways to make it through your day when you feel like there is too much to do.

One thing you can do is to organize your day. This will allow you to attack the day with a plan. This will also help you stay organized, and your mind won't feel rushed.

If you are organized, then you will be able to stay focused on one task at a time. It will allow the rest of the tasks to get done more easily. It won't feel like there is so much happening at once.

Start your day by making a list of everything you need to do that day. You can even create lists for each task if it makes it easier.

Another thing that can help is to set realistic expectations for yourself. Many people with ADHD are prone to setting expectations that are too high. This can be harmful to you because it can cause you to feel like the day is rushed and like everything is falling apart. Start small by only setting one expectation at a time.

Another thing that helps is to learn to make good decisions, and to take your time doing so. Many people with ADHD feel like they need to rush when it is decision time. Then when they make a decision, they end up regretting it. You also need to learn how to say no in certain situations. This one step alone will help dramatically.

If you do find yourself feeling overwhelmed, take a moment to slow down. If possible, find a quiet space where you can sit alone and relax. Listen to music, close your eyes, or take a nap.

This can be difficult because you may feel like there is no time to slow down. When your day feels rushed, you might feel like this relaxing time is almost impolite. But if you can sit alone for even one minute, it can help you find peace.

Don't compromise your health in order to get everything done!

Sometimes not getting it all done can be better than trying to do too much. This is especially true of ADHD. When you push yourself too hard, you're going to end up making mistakes and feeling like a failure. This can really harm your self-esteem and can make it harder to work effectively the next day.

If you know you can't get everything done at work, it is okay to tell your boss. If he or she doesn't want to hear it, then find a different job. But you may find they are willing to compromise on deadlines.

What It Means to Be a Leader

When you're a leader, it can be easy to feel like you must know everything about every aspect of your business because people look up to you and listen to what you say. But this can be very overwhelming for people with ADHD. It can also be very tempting for leaders with ADHD to want to rush through their tasks.

When you're leading your company, you need to remember that there's no rush. If you rush through the tasks at hand, you'll likely do a terrible job and feel overwhelmed.

When you're trying to lead your team, it's also important to give them as much time as they need. It may be tempting for you to rush through your work and then push your employees to also finish their work quickly, but if they feel rushed then they won't perform to the best of their abilities.

It may be really difficult to let go of some tasks and allow someone else take the lead. This kind of leadership is kind of like parenting. When children are young, they need so much support and a lot of help from their parents. But as they grow up, they will become more independent.

At some point your team will become independent too. You can then let them take the lead and trust their abilities.

Sometimes the best thing for your team is to let people know that they need to take on more responsibilities. You can then tell them that they will be rewarded for working hard and helping out in the office. This way they see that their success is your success too.

You can also try assigning tasks according to who deserves them most instead of just handing them off to whomever happens get their hands on the task first.

These are some of the ways that you can be your own best leader.

Overcoming Fear of Failure

Many people who have ADHD will approach tasks or projects with a great deal of fear. These fears are often not based on reality and will end up creating a sense of inadequacy for the person with ADHD.

Some fear that if they fail at something, their whole life is going to be ruined. They also fear that if they do not succeed, the person might think they are stupid or weak, which is an even bigger threat.

People who suffer from ADHD often have a high need for approval and a low level of self-esteem. They often look to others for their validation and worth, which can make them afraid of what others will say about them if they make a mistake.

It also makes them anxious because they want to be liked by other people. They want other people to feel as though they are worth something.

If we find ourselves feeling as though we cannot do something because of the fear of failure, it is important that we change this type of thinking as soon as possible. We need to recognize that everyone fails at some point in their lives and those who succeed use those failures for motivation.

Those who do not fear failure are much more likely to succeed in their endeavors. They need to believe in themselves and know they can accomplish anything that they set their mind to. When we stop focusing on the outcome of our endeavors, it becomes easier for us realize that failure is not the end of the world.

When we start focusing on the outcome of something, it can cause us to become more anxiety ridden and this often leads to even more procrastination. The more we fear failure, the more likely we are to procrastinate. The more we focus on the outcome of a project or task, the less motivated we become.

The initial step to overcoming this fear is to realize that it is an irrational fear and not based on reality. Try to think about other things that can go wrong in your life and see if those things actually happen. The next time you feel as though you cannot do something because of your fear of failure, change your thinking as soon as possible.

Remember, all individuals fail at some point in their lives. You do not need to be defined by these failures. When you take a moment to think about all the times that you have succeeded rather than failed, it will help ease your fear of failure. When you focus on the positive, it can help decrease your anxiety and increase your confidence.

CHAPTER 10: MANAGING ANXIETY-INDUCING WORKPLACE SITUATIONS

Most people with ADHD have a difficult time working in certain environments. In many cases, these environments can cause anxiety for those who experience them.

When we are working in an environment that causes us to feel anxious, we can become distracted and forgetful. We will often push ourselves harder in order to get the job done, but that is not always possible.

If you find yourself feeling anxious at work or school, try to identify what it is that is causing you anxiety. You can then try changing your mindset or taking a break. Anxiety is often the result of not paying enough attention to what you are doing. It can also be caused by the way people around you act or react to your behavior.

Take some time to think about how you can change your environment so it does not cause you anxiety. Remember, anxiety is not good for your productivity and performance at work or school.

Try listening to music or doing some deep breathing exercises to calm yourself down. Take a short walk or grab some tea. When we are experiencing anxiety, it is important to try and calm ourselves down as quickly as possible. If we allow our anxiety to get the best of us, it can cause us to make mistakes or to forget things that we need to do.

Remember, anxiety can cause you to become distracted and unfocused. Think about what might be causing your anxiety and do your best to avoid it.

Time Management for Adult ADHD

Time management is a key ADHD-related strategy because it helps you plan, organize and make the most of your time. It often makes projects easier to accomplish and can help keep you on track with daily activities.

Incomplete tasks can create frustration, stress, and feelings of being overwhelmed. These feelings lead to procrastination or avoidance, which can then affect your relationships at home or work.

For most people, time management helps them identify and solve problems. It helps you plan effectively and get on track with your plans. It can also help you to increase your productivity and create the most value from the time you have on a daily basis. Management is a proactive skill that needs to be learned and used on a daily basis. Planning and management become most effective when you strive to develop discipline and dedication. There is no better strategy than utilizing the time you have available.

Effective Time Management Strategies for Adults with ADHD

Planning for the next day or week is vital. Whether you are at work or in your personal life, it is important to plan ahead to make sure you are on top of things. When you plan ahead , you can control what you do and how much time it will take to accomplish the task. Use a time management planner or calendar to write out your daily activities well in advance. Keep a log of all the important tasks that need to be accomplished during the day. You can have a running list of all deadlines and appointments as well as plans for the coming week. Create a goal plan that specifies how you want to use your time. It can be helpful to include targets for daily, weekly, monthly, yearly, and long-term goals. When you keep a running list of all of your tasks and deadlines, the task of analyzing your priorities will become easier.

Once you have a plan for the day, it is important to write it down. The process of writing down your tasks and goals will help give them more importance and make them feel more realistic. Create a daily to-do list with things you will be doing throughout the day. Put the most important tasks at the top of this list. Then write down any other activities that need attention. Next, come up with a priority system that will help you prioritize your daily tasks. Put tasks in order according to what needs to get done first. In other words, your "A" tasks need to be completed before your "B" and "C" tasks.

Once you have a very clear idea of what needs to be done, the work of prioritizing and planning becomes easier. You can then schedule your "A" items during the most productive time of the day while completing your less important tasks during other less busy times. For most individuals, this is the best way to organize your personal and working life.

Long-term planning is especially important for adults with ADHD because it helps them stay on track with important tasks throughout the year. It also helps them avoid the consequences of procrastination. When you have a plan for the coming week, month or year, it is easier to decide how you will use your time. In order to have a great quality of life, it is important to think about your future needs and the needs of others. An effective long-term plan for ADHD adults is to create goals that are realistic and attainable. It should include goals in your career field, school, or community activities.

It is essential to set goals that are measurable. Setting goals where you can see progress can help you stay motivated and on track. When the goals feel unattainable, it can be hard to maintain motivation. Once the goals are accomplished, once again, it becomes easier to maintain motivation.

If you learn how to prioritize and work with a time management plan, you will feel better about your day and be able to accomplish more in less time. Once again, the key is discipline and dedication. Strive for consistency in following through with all of your plans.

Time Management

Step 1: Write down on one sheet of paper the things you want to accomplish today.

1...____

2...____

3...____

4...____

Step 2: Set a time limit for each task. Write the time needed to complete each job below.

1...____

2...____

3...____

4...____

Step 3: Consider how you could use your time more efficiently for this event/task/mission/project/etc.. Write down three options that would allow you to accomplish this task in a more efficient manner:

1...____

2...____

3...____

4...____

Step 4: What steps can you take to accomplish this list? Write down how you can accomplish these goals and tasks below:

1...____

2...____

3...____

4...____

Step 5: What will happen if you are not able to meet your goals today? Write down the consequences of not being able to complete this list:

1...____

2...____

3...____

4...____

Step 6: What are three things that are outside your control? Write those down below:

1...____

2...____

3...____

4...____

Step 7: If you did not meet your goals or accomplish what you wanted to do today, write down why below:

1...____

2...____

3...____

4...____

To stay focused on your goals, I suggest you make a timetable each month, each week, and each day for what you want to accomplish. This can help keep you focused on your tasks for the day so you can meet all your deadlines and avoid procrastination. It will also reduce the amount of stress that comes with losing time or not accomplishing what you wanted to do.

Time management is essential to success. If you make a plan and stick to it, you will be amazed at how much more you can accomplish.

Workplace Issues

ADHD can cause daytime fatigue, trouble concentrating, and insomnia. The condition often leads to high levels of irritability and mood swings. However, many adults with ADHD still work successfully in the workplace. It's really important to note that not all people with ADHD will experience such problems, and not everyone who has a job-related issue is diagnosed with ADHD.

Several factors can contribute to the difficulties experienced by adults with ADHD in the workplace. These include:

1. Inattention and Distractibility

Inattention can result in missing important details or being unable to concentrate on a task for a long period of time. This lapse, in turn, can cause a person to miss deadlines and fail to meet expectations.

Daily distractions at work can compound the impact of such difficulties. A person with ADHD might be more easily distracted by things like the sound of a loud machine in the next cubicle, something flashing across his or her computer screen, or an arguing couple walking by.

2. Organizational Difficulties

Problems with time management and organization can make it hard for some people to be productive at work. They may find it difficult to organize their workspace, meet deadlines, complete work assignments on time, keep track of files and records, and properly file paperwork on time.

3. Sociability and Interaction Difficulties

ADHD occurs along a wide spectrum, and not everyone who has the condition is socially awkward or shy. However, when people with ADHD do have problems in these areas, it can be much more noticeable than when other people do. Such individuals may talk to others in a disorganized manner or interrupt others' conversations. They may sit in their cubicles alone without interacting much with others. They may also be reluctant to participate in social activities. He or she may also have trouble working well with others and be overly critical of others' work. The ADHD individual may also have problems meeting people, greeting them appropriately, remembering their names, and interacting with them smoothly.

These difficulties make it difficult to develop and maintain relationships with others on a personal level at work. They may not know how to properly initiate and participate in conversations and meetings, and they may be very self-conscious regarding their speech and appearance. Other employees may assume that such individuals are socially awkward or lack social skills, which often leads to them being rejected for promotion or hiring.

4. Workplace Bullying

When work environments are hostile, bullying can occur. Workplace bullying is defined as any offensive behavior that happens in the workplace, whether verbal or nonverbal, that intentionally hurts an employee's dignity or sense of self-worth. This behavior can range from teasing to outright abuse, which ranges from threatening language to physical assaults. Bullying at work can cause great emotional pain for people with ADHD.

5. Poor Self-Esteem and Social Skills

Many people with ADHD experience problems with their self-esteem and social skills. If someone feels shame or embarrassment about his or her ADHD symptoms, this can cause additional problems at work. Such individuals might not be able to express themselves well verbally, and their actions may be viewed as strange or even potentially dangerous by other employees.

6. Poor Auditory and Visual Processing

Some people with ADHD have problems with visual and auditory processing, which can cause them to misunderstand the information they receive from written words, electronic media, and spoken language. They may not remember what they read, so they may need to reread information presented to them or may need to take notes during a meeting or class. They might not be able to sort out the main ideas from supporting details when reading. And such individuals may not be able to understand spoken language well enough to follow a conversation.

Since many people take their cues from others' understanding or expressions during a conversation, ADHD individuals may not be able to receive all the necessary information from an interaction.

7. Poor Working Memory and Distractibility

Research has suggested that adults with ADHD have trouble storing or keeping information in their working memory long enough to use it. Someone with this problem might be unable to remember information from a previous meeting, instructions from a supervisor, or specifics about a project he or she is working on. In addition, some ADHD individuals may be more distractible than others because their minds are always going in many different directions at once.

8. Poor Mathematical Skills

Some people with ADHD have trouble understanding or doing mathematical calculations. They sometimes struggle to follow the logic of a mathematical problem or understand the meaning of numbers. Since many jobs require some amount of calculation, this can create problems for people with ADHD.

9. Difficulty with Decision Making

Research has indicated that the information-processing system of people with ADHD may be different from that of people without the condition. The brain's ability to seek and consider new information and make connections between different pieces of information may be inefficient in people with ADHD, which can cause some problems when making decisions. Consequently, some ADHD individuals may not be able to generate enough options to choose from when faced with a problem or task for which they need to make a decision. They also might become stuck on one option and not consider other possibilities. This makes it so difficult for them to make decisions, especially when they are working on new or unfamiliar tasks.

10. Impulsivity

People with ADHD may have difficulty waiting for their turn to speak in a conversation, interrupting others' conversations, blurting out inappropriate comments or questions, and acting without thinking about the consequences. Such individuals often are seen as impulsive or aggressive. They might say or do things without considering how they might be perceived by others.

Getting a Good Job with ADHD

Those who are living with ADHD are much more likely to have a difficult time finding the right type of job. They need to look at ways that they can improve themselves in order to get better jobs in the future.

Success is not easy to come by if you do not put in a lot of effort. When we focus our attention on the outcome of a situation, it can trigger anxiety and distract us from the things we need to accomplish. Many people with ADHD end up working in jobs they hate because they simply do not have the ability to focus their attention on the job at hand.

Anyone living with ADHD should remember that they need to pay attention to the things that are happening around them. The more you know and learn about yourself and your triggers, the easier it will be for you to live a successful life.

When you take time to understand your own strengths and weaknesses, it will be much easier for you find a job that works well for you. Keep trying until you find something that fits well with your strengths and weaknesses.

Getting into College with ADHD

College is a time of enormous growth. You are suddenly thrown into an environment where you have the freedom to develop through your own means, experiment with different career paths and complete the degree that best fits your needs. For most people, college is a challenging but ultimately rewarding experience.

However, for those that suffer from ADHD symptoms in adulthood, it can be a lot more complicated. Sometimes, you may feel like the whole world is against you. You'll feel like everyone has expectations of who you are or who they want you to become and nothing feels right. It's hard to figure out where to turn for help and it can feel like there's no one who can relate to what you're going through.

The best way to approach college with ADHD symptoms is to break things down into smaller steps that aren't as overwhelming. Talk with someone who has gone through the experience and learn from their successes and mistakes. Getting insight from those who have been there will make it a lot easier to set goals and create achievable milestones.

There are some steps you can take to make your college experience as smooth as possible, but first you need to understand how ADHD symptoms will affect your time at college and why you need to plan ahead. The following are just some suggestions that may help you get started.

1. *ADHD is not an excuse*

The first thing to realize is that ADHD is not an excuse for not doing well in college. You'll need to learn some new strategies to cope with the challenges you'll face.

Your new strategies may include making some adjustments so you can better manage your time. For example, you might prioritize certain tasks so you don't find yourself overwhelmed or overextended. You'll also need to learn what you can control and what you can't.

It's also important to realize that there are so many distractions in college, including all the new people, events and opportunities.

2. Learn to work through difficulties

It's very important to learn how to deal with the challenges that school and college throw at you, and you can't do that by withdrawing and hiding. The more you can get involved and engaged in things, the better off you will be.

3. Manage your time wisely

You need to find a way to manage your time and be sure that you're not overcommitting yourself. It can be so tempting to say yes to everything because it feels good in the moment and you want everyone to like you. You also want to feel like you belong and are an important part of the group. But when things get busy, it may become difficult to meet all your obligations and complete your assignments.

5. Allow time for yourself

Another essential thing to learn is not to neglect yourself while you're trying to get everything done. Study, do your homework, volunteer and be involved in campus organizations, but also make time for yourself. Find activities that are fun and relaxing. Be sure to get enough sleep and eat well.

6. Be open to criticism

It's really important to be open to criticism because it can help you grow as both an individual and a member of the group. It's easy to feel defensive when someone else criticizes you, but it's important to listen to whatever they have to say because there may be some truth there.

7. Avoid high-stakes situations

High-stakes situations can be some of the most difficult ones to deal with, especially if you're a person with ADHD. When someone's grade depends on your performance, it's hard to avoid the anxiety and stress that come with that responsibility. Not only will you feel pressure from yourself but from your teachers and parents as well. Avoiding this kind of situation is not always possible, but with proper planning, you can make sure that it won't overwhelm you.

8. Prioritize your most important tasks

It is important to prioritize your tasks so you don't lose sight of the big picture. Some of your most important tasks may be to keep on top of your homework, take care of your health and wellness, focus on schoolwork and socialize with friends.

9. Establish a support system

Make sure you have people that are willing to help you when you are in need. Get the support that you need when it comes to being on time, doing homework, and getting rest. It's easy to feel isolated when dealing with ADHD symptoms in adulthood and this can lead to depression.

10. Give yourself the gift of boundaries

It's important to have boundaries. Make sure to have downtime for yourself so you can relax and unwind. You will need to focus on what you should be doing instead of worrying about other things. If you focus on the task at hand first it should be easier for you to get other things done as well.

CHAPTER 11: ADULT ADHD AND ITS IMPACT ON ROMANTIC RELATIONSHIPS

When we live with ADHD, it can be difficult to maintain healthy relationships. It can cause us to become extremely distracted and it often causes us to feel as though we are not good enough for our partners.

If you do experience relationship problems because of your ADHD, it is important to take a step back and then think about the relationship as whole. Although your ADHD may cause some issues in your relationship, there may be other factors at play that you might not realize.

Take some time to think about what your ADHD might be causing in your relationship and try to figure out if there is something else going on. If you are living with ADHD, you will probably need to have some sort of conversation with your partner about it.

It is important for you to be able to communicate with your partner in a way that allows both of you to express yourselves. Remember, emotions are another thing that many people hide from people they care about.

When we feel as though we can no longer hide our emotions, we may end up not knowing how to deal with them. When that happens, it can cause us to feel as though we are nothing and that no one will ever love us.

Be sure to always keep the lines of communication open and spend time getting to know yourself and your partner. Make sure that your relationship with yourself is healthy before you spend time improving your relationship with those around you.

Thinking About Marriage?

Many people who struggle with ADHD feel anxious about the idea of marriage. They fear they'll be too irresponsible to manage a family, or their hyperactivity will make raising children difficult.

There's no reason to believe the ADHD brain is less capable of being a good parent or spouse than anyone else's. In fact, research shows that some people with ADHD actually do better in marriage than people without ADHD. They tend to be more committed, affectionate, and dedicated to the relationship.

If you're thinking about marriage, it's a good idea to explore your concerns in a structured way with a therapist or coach. A therapist can help you identify the roots of your negative feelings about marriage, and help you work on them. A coach can help you plan for a fulfilling marriage and provide support as the day approaches.

Here are some common concerns people with ADHD have about marriage:

Anxiety about Finances

One of the most common concerns about getting married is money, especially if one or both partners has ADHD and struggles with spending and budgeting.

You may worry that you can't manage money together or that you'll be tempted to keep separate bank accounts.

Both of these things are very doable. In fact, keeping separate accounts is a good idea for any ADHD couple. It prevents the situation where one partner takes control over the other's spending, and it also keeps both partners from feeling guilty when one gives in to a spending binge. Make an agreement that any "spending" money is the partner's individual responsibility.

A therapist or coach may help you develop spending plans you can both commit to, and figure out what works best for you. If budgeting makes you anxious, consider using software or a smartphone app to keep track of your spending.

Lack of Responsibility & Task-Overspacing

People with ADHD are notorious for being late or not showing up at all.

You'll have to develop good habits for saying "no" when you're overwhelmed with other tasks, and for making sure each partner has enough time in the day to do what he or she needs to do. This sounds simple, but it isn't always easy. You need to learn how to say "no" and how to take time for yourself without guilt.

You may also want to work on your internalized responses. The following statements aren't helpful: "I've never been able to get anything done," or, "I'm bad at this." They do not inspire the motivation you need to make good habits part of your daily routine.

Instead, try a positive self-statement like, "I can do it," or, "It's in my power. I'm going to get it done. No excuses, no delays." You can even make a comment card to yourself to remind yourself of this positive outlook.

Lack of Commitment & Lack of Trust

People with ADHD often struggle with commitment issues. They may fear they'll be too unreliable to commit to marriage.

It may be hard to tell whether fear of commitment is the issue. An ADHD coach or therapist may help you explore the reasons for your reluctance to commit. It may also be valuable to do a commitment ceremony with your partner to make promises about your relationship if these fears are still present after counseling.

It's also important that you address these issues proactively, before a trusting relationship has a chance to grow.

Lack of Emotional Attachment & Lack of Intimacy

People with ADHD frequently struggle with feelings of isolation and aloneness. They may fear any sort of intimacy will make them vulnerable to having their needs unmet by someone else. They may also feel uncomfortable with physical intimacy, or worry that they won't be able to meet the needs of their partner.

A therapist or coach can help you explore these issues and work on them with a structured practice. You might also want to learn some techniques for feeling more comfortable with touch and emotion.

Anxiety About the Future

People with ADHD may fear that they will be unable to plan for the future or that they won't be able to stay committed to a long-term relationship. They may also feel overwhelmed and anxious about making decisions about their lives.

The best way to get past these issues is to take them one at a time, and start small. Start planning for the future: setting your budget, planning for retirement and healthcare, and planning how you want to spend your free time.

It's worth putting in some real work to get these things down on paper. You won't even feel like you're committing too much if you can pull off a small success with these steps.

Fear of Success & Fear of Failure

Recognize that there will be challenges in any marriage. A good marriage helps you learn to deal with those challenges so they don't overwhelm you.

The challenges your partner will face may be a little different from the ones you deal with every day, but they're likely to come from the same issues of anxiety and fear.

A coach or therapist can help you explore these feelings and work through them so they don't stop your relationship from growing. You can also work on learning how to be more comfortable making mistakes and learning from them.

How to Manage ADHD Symptoms as a Spouse

When a person has ADHD, their spouse often has to adapt their own life to accommodate. By following these tips for managing your spouse's ADHD symptoms, you can reduce friction and increase the quality of your relationship.

As a spouse of someone with ADHD, you probably feel like you are always taking on most of the household responsibilities. You might be so tired of feeling like you are working at cross purposes to your partner. You may feel like one or both of you are often short on patience or lacking in intimacy. You may even feel like you are not emotionally or physically attracted to your spouse. You may feel like you are constantly nagging, correcting, or making allowances. These feelings are not unusual.

All these feelings will go away if the ADHD symptoms are properly treated and managed, but that doesn't mean that it is always easy to change the situation. It may mean that one of you has to make some serious changes in your life, and accept some temporary discomfort for long-term improvement.

As a spouse of someone with ADHD, you may need to make some sacrifices or even take on some extra duties in order for the relationship to function better. You cannot change your spouse's ADHD symptoms, but you can help manage them.

Have patience not just with yourself and your spouse, but also with yourself as a spouse. This means being more understanding and forgiving of the challenges your ADHD partner presents to you. It could also means that you will have to be a source of comfort and reassurance even when you feel anxious or tense.

For example, if your spouse has a tendency to forget appointments, but frequently resents you for calling to remind them, try to be as patient as possible.

Be aware of ADHD triggers such as the heating or air conditioning turning off, or a clock ticking, and be prepared to ask your spouse frequently if they are okay. The more frequently you do this, the better prepared you will be to help them when the trigger happens.

Do not give up easily and do not be impatient with yourself. Allow for the time it takes for your spouse to respond if they give you any trouble or are slow to reply. Remember, talking is often helpful, so try to be patient.

Do not give up if your spouse seems reluctant or unable to accept help from family members or friends, even though they may have offered it many times.

Have realistic expectations of yourself as a spouse. Be willing to compromise and try not to put off difficult tasks for later.

Never expect your spouse to change their behavior on a daily or even an hour-to-hour basis. If they are very late, ask them what they can do differently next time if they want to change. You may need to make some changes in your own schedule, such as working from home.

Try to avoid tasking your ADHD partner with tasks that are not their responsibility. However, be aware of any tricks your ADHD partner uses to get out of things they need to be doing. It is okay to ask them if they are okay or if they need any help, but try not to be bossy or nag them about their mistakes. If you have the natural tendency to criticize or correct your spouse, try to catch yourself.

Try not to speak in a hurried or angry tone. Remember that there is no need to make them feel bad about taking too long or for asking you for help.

Do not take it personally if your spouse does not seem to remember everything you tell them. Have the expectation that they will do what you ask, but do not expect them to remember everything that you've said.

Please, please, please never stress yourself out by trying to save money for your ADHD partner! Do save money if you can, but don't feel like you have to take on this responsibility by yourself. Your spouse will only feel more shame and guilt over their symptoms if they are unable to contribute financially.

How to Handle Arguments

Anger is just a normal human emotion, and it can serve us in some situations. However, anger management is essential for adults who have ADHD or are married to an adult with ADHD because anger can have serious consequences for the family – especially if the person with ADHD has a very poor impulse control and low frustration tolerance. Learning to control anger and its consequences is a critical factor in the management of ADHD. Here are some basic rules for having effective arguments with children, friends, or other adults.

1. Discuss the problem with the concerned person. It can be very hard to stay calm when things are not going your way. It may help to turn the argument into

a discussion about the problem you are having. This can help get to the heart of what is really bothering you or the other person and allow you to work towards a solution.

2. Think about what you want from this argument before engaging in it. If possible, try to identify why this argument is so important for you. Are you trying to make a point? Are you simply trying to get information from the other person? Are you trying to change the other person's behavior? Whatever your goal is, always keep it in mind as you work towards a solution.

3. Always listen to what the other person has to say. Try not to interrupt the other person as they state their point of view. You may find that the other person is just as confused as you are about what is happening, and you may find yourself agreeing with some of the things they say.

4. State your own opinions and feelings in a calm, objective manner. Most people will want to know what you think and feel after listening to their perspective. Take turns sharing your opinions and feelings. It can be very hard to listen totally objectively to another person's opinion. But it's important to give each other the chance to speak before you interject with your own thoughts and opinions.

5. Listen carefully and think before responding. Listen to the other person's point of view without interrupting him or her, and then respond with a statement that agrees or disagrees. It is important to listen more than you talk when discussing a problem, but do not shy away from being assertive if you disagree on a particular issue.

6. Be clear about what you are expecting from the resolution to the argument. Try not to get into a fight for the sake of fighting or because you are angry with each other or want to punish him/her for something he or she has said or done.

7. Agree to disagree. Sometimes, despite your best efforts, you can find that you have different opinions on an issue and there is no way to meet in the middle. This can be frustrating, but it is important not to get bogged down in the argument.

8. Expect change. If you talk about issues often, you are more likely to learn something new about the other person in the process. Try to incorporate this information into your next conversation with your partner or friend in an effort to develop a deeper understanding of their personality and behavior.

Relationships and Marriage: The Downside of Hyper-focus

If you're a person with ADHD, you may be having trouble finding the right person to share your life with. Or, if you're married or in a committed relationship, you may feel that the person falls short of meeting many of your criteria for a good partner.

The reality is that marriage can bring its own set of challenges for those with ADHD, but there are some advantages as well. Here are 10 tips for people who are trying to find love:

Set your own bar for who is a good match

Since ADHD can make it hard to maintain relationships, you'll want to find someone who shares your interests, is willing to communicate openly and honestly, and has a good work ethic. You should also look for someone who will take into account the extra challenges you have in your life, including behavioral problems that have been tough to manage. The most essential thing is that you know what you're looking for in a partner yourself. Then, you can start to look at people who might fit the bill.

There's no perfect person for us

While there are some common traits among people with ADHD, it's important to realize that there is no one single personality type that will work best in a relationship. This means that when you meet a person, you should not be looking at them and thinking "this is the one." Instead, you should try to find a person who has a lot in common with you and has complementary traits to your own personality.

Actively seek out different situations that will challenge you

It can be helpful to date someone who is likely to challenge you. This allows you to try out new things together, such as watching movies for hours on end, going on road trips, attending concerts and sporting events.

It can really help you learn more about your partner when you're challenged by what's happening. For example, when you go to a concert with someone who is an avid fan of that kind of music, you'll want to pay attention and make sure you understand the nuances and relevance of the lyrics in relation to the music itself. This is a perfect time to talk through what you're seeing and how it relates to the band's overall message with your significant other.

Work with your partner to learn the rules of each other's ADHD

Sometimes life with a person who has ADHD can be very frustrating. One of the most crucial things you can do for your relationship is to recognize that it's not only helpful but necessary for you to understand how your significant other is organized. When they are working on something, it will be helpful for you to know what they need in order to stay focused.

It's also important for you to realize that your partner might have different ways of doing things to you. For example, a person with ADHD may need extra time to organize a project before they can get started. It's important that you learn to accommodate one another's needs.

Be aware of your own ADHD behaviors

Many people with ADHD will want to make sure that they are not causing problems in their relationship. But this is rarely possible, since you can't change who you are. The best that you can do is to recognize when things aren't working, and then find ways to change the things that don't work for you and your partner.

One of the easiest ways to do this is by recognizing your own ADHD behaviors, such as not paying attention in conversations, forgetting where things are placed in a room, and getting distracted easily. Many people with ADHD will try to minimize their own problems while placing blame on the actions of their partner.

Find ways for each of you to be involved in decision-making

It's important to recognize when it's best to speak up about something. However, it's most important that both of you feel comfortable in all aspects of your life together. Part of finding the right partner is finding out what aspects of their household they want to run their own way. This means that you should ask them about what they want to do about paying bills, cleaning the house, eating meals, and other similar issues. For example, you may want to learn who was doing the laundry before you entered their life. This can help prevent conflict in the future by making sure that both of you are on the same page.

It's also important for your partner to let you know what kind of help they'll need from time to time. For example, they might need some help with the TV remote when it's time for bed. Or maybe there are moments when they'll want to take care of their own finances, but you can offer them help with paperwork or organizing their documents.

Don't try to change the habits of someone with ADHD

Remember that habits are very important for your partner. Breaking them will often cause them to feel frustrated and disorganized at the same time. It's important for both of you to find ways to work around the habits that are difficult to change. You can accomplish this by being flexible when it comes to the things that your partner likes. For example, if your significant other needs somewhere quiet in order to get their homework done, you should be respectful of their need to have a space of their own.

Don't let ADHD take over everything

Sometimes ADHD can lead people into making bad decisions that create problems between themselves and other people. For instance, a person with ADHD may have an impulse to spend a lot of money on things they don't need, and you'll want to keep a close eye on this.

Make sure that ADHD does not take over everything. ADHD can cause people to act impulsively rather than wisely. Help your partner understand that there are other ways to make decisions that will avoid conflict.

Stop Fighting and Start Communicating

Want to make your relationship last forever? Here are some simple ways...

Know what communication style your partner prefers. People with ADHD are often impatient, that's why communication is very important. It helps if you are good at asking questions. Get to know each other's problems and concerns by asking them.

Remember to use "I" statements in a relationship. There's a huge difference between saying "you always leave the toothpaste messy" and expressing yourself from an emotion point of view, for example, "When I walk into the bathroom, I'm frustrated when I see that you have left it messy. I don't like to see my stuff looking messy."

If something bad happens, don't blame each other for not communicating. Always communicate openly. Be patient with each other, take things slowly. Try to be understanding of your partner's demands or needs because they are just as valid as yours.

When you agree on something that you want to do together, stick with it. Be honest with your partner, because lying will only make it harder to maintain the relationship. Don't hold anything back from your partner, as this can make them feel insecure.

Try to think outside the box when it comes to your relationship. Try activities that make you happier and be more loving towards each other. Show love and care every day. This is important for successful relationships in general, and it can be challenging when one or both of you have ADHD. When you secure the love and commitment of your partner, it helps you to be more patient.

Try not to get into angry arguments or fights. If differences in opinion are brought up, try to agree on compromises instead of fighting. Try to avoid arguing when you are both angry. Recognize the red flags that your partner may give. If your significant other is angry at you, don't ignore the signals. Talk about the cause of their anger and work towards resolving it. If you know that you can't handle certain situations or people, make sure to tell your partner. Identifying triggers in advance will help you both be more prepared when dealing with them. Never give up on each other.

Trust and commitment can help you and your partner learn how to talk about your feelings and problems together. When there is trust, there's a lot of value in the relationship. If you can't trust one another completely, it will be very hard for you to be honest about things that are important. Be honest with yourself when it comes to your relationship, because having ADHD can make it difficult to know what you truly want in your life.

Spend time on your relationship. Schedule time to be together and make the most of it. Let your partner know the things you value about them and show them the same amount of appreciation and respect as they give you. Always remember that in order for a relationship to work, both partners need to want the same things in life. When you don't know what you really want or where you're going in life, it will be very difficult to maintain a successful relationship.

Use these ideas and techniques and improve your relationship and keep the love alive!

Having ADHD means we have many challenges. Especially when it comes to couples, things can get a little complicated. When we have ADHD, our capacity for relationships is affected because the way we think and communicate may be different from most people. We can often forget that other people have their own difficulties but still wish to have a relationship with us. This is why some of us suffer from feeling neglected or even abused at times by partners who have no idea how to communicate effectively. But this doesn't mean that we are necessarily with the wrong people. It's all a matter of communication.

Because we take things very literally, we can sometimes make mistakes and make assumptions about what others really want from us, assuming that they mean just what they say. We might take everything people say as a personal attack and misunderstand their motives, which can lead to unnecessary conflicts.

When we have ADHD, it can be hard to know what we want and who we really love. But when we communicate effectively with others, we make sure they understand what's important. It's important to make sure that our partner knows what we mean and the reason for our actions as it will help them know if we're being unfair or not. For example, we need to be clear about what we mean when we say that we're "angry" or "upset." We need to be very clear with other people about how we truly feel. When we communicate effectively, others can follow along with what's going on in our heads.

ADHD people live with others, they often have trouble communicating their thoughts and feelings to them. This can lead to misunderstandings in relationships. When it comes to relationships, people need to know when something is important and what the other person wants at all times. This can be hard for people with ADHD and can create a lot of unnecessary problems in their relationships.

It's important that the person you love understands your problems and supports you through them. When we communicate effectively, we can be more successful and happier in our relationships. We're less likely to feel lonely and more likely to be accepted for who we are. The more you try to reach out and talk about your problems, the happier you will be.

If you're not used to communicating effectively with others, then try some of these suggestions: Give each other more time to talk. Try listening more often than talking. Make sure that what you say is clear at all times, by not using words or expressions that are hard to understand. Be careful not to assume that the other person understands what you mean. Talk about your feelings and try to be as honest as you can at all times.

CHAPTER 12: COPING WITH LOW MOOD AND DEPRESSION

In this chapter, we look at the effects that chronic stress has on our lives and how to deal with these feelings. We also focus on ADHD coping skills for when you're feeling down or depressed.

"I'm so frustrated all of the time." "I feel like I'm constantly behind and everyone is passing me by." "My life feels hopeless and I can't seem to do anything right." These are some common statements adults with ADHD hear from their partners and friends. It can be very frustrating for the loved ones to witness their ADHD partner's struggles. They become disheartened when they try to help, only to see that no matter what is tried, nothing seems to work. And then they start thinking that perhaps the person with ADHD isn't trying hard enough.

Many partners feel resentful towards their ADHD partners because they know how capable and talented they are in many other areas of life. It's so hard to see someone you love struggle so much in one specific area of their life. So the focus of the relationship begins to shift. Instead of enjoying your partner's talents and strengths, their weaknesses seem to loom large.

It's important to understand that dealing with chronic stress has a significant impact on our moods and how we feel about ourselves.

How Chronic Stress Affects Us

People often assume that if something is difficult it should also be painful, but this isn't necessarily true. The stress of a situation, or a problem to be dealt with, can take a toll on our psyches but it doesn't always have to be painful. The reactions we have to stressors are different for every person, and the intensity of the reactions depends on how much we're trying to deal with the situation.

If we just try to check out from stressors that aren't too threatening, then they don't have much of an impact on us. However, if we are actively engaged in dealing with the stressor, it can have a negative effect on our emotions.

When the source of the stressor is constantly present in our lives, constantly being dealt with in some way, there are serious consequences for our overall moods. Even when nothing is being actively done to deal with the stressor, it's always there to be thought about and worried about. It's like a permanently running faucet in your bathroom that never gets turned off.

Many people with ADHD have a very difficult time just "chilling out." They can tend to be very active, constantly thinking about what's going on and how to deal with it. This adds to their stress and causes them to become overwhelmed.

ADHD can make us feel like we're constantly under pressure. We feel like we're behind on everything and that there is never enough time to do things, go places, or do the things we need to do. We all have different things that get in the way of our plans, and they can sometimes seem too big to deal with.

It's important to remember that the reason there are so many things vying for our attention is because of ADHD. Even though we may already know this, it can still be hard to acknowledge that this is the source of our constant stress.

Why Stress Builds Up

The following are some common causes of chronic stress. Think about whether they apply to you:

Urgent tasks, ongoing problems, and unexpected circumstances – for example, not having enough money or time to deal with a life situation, or needing to deal with an ongoing problem such as a child who isn't doing well at school

- Not knowing what you need to do – for example, having too many things that need to be done and not knowing what to prioritize

- Large amounts of unstructured time

- Failure – for example, being unsuccessful at some task or not being able to develop some skill or ability even though you have been trying for a long time

- Inability to cope –stressful situations you're unable to deal with

- Feeling as though you have no options – if you can't think of a way out of a situation and thus feel trapped, this will cause significant stress on your emotional well-being.

The best way to deal with stress is by reducing your exposure to these situations. Unfortunately, one of the biggest problems people with ADHD face is that they don't know how to eliminate their exposure. Before you can do so, you need to identify exactly what is causing the stress in your life. Though it may be impossible to eliminate stress entirely, you can reduce and control how much it affects you.

Everyone feels stressed at some time or another. If the reason for the stress is something that happened in the past and there is nothing more we can do about it, we need to let go of our feelings about it and move on with our lives. The things that cause stress now are the things we need to worry about. We only have so much energy to allocate to each of our stresses, so we need to choose wisely.

Chronic Stress and ADHD

Everyone who has ADHD feels stressed much of the time. Find out how much chronic stress affects your life by reading through this list and seeing how many of these apply to you:

- It's hard for me to feel relaxed and at ease.

- I feel nervous or on edge.

- I always feel like I'm on the run.

- I'm always in a hurry.

- It's hard for me to relax and slow down.

- It's hard for me to make good decisions about how to spend my time.

- It's hard for me to think about things that need to be done, although I know they are there.

- I often have too much to do.

- There's so much going on, I don't know what to do.

- I have a hard time just being in one place or not doing something.

- I struggle to relax and let go.

- I'm a disorganized person and can't seem to get anything done.

- I worry about having enough time and energy for everything that needs to be done.

- I'm not as successful as I would like to be.

- I don't feel as successful as others think I am.

- It's hard for me to keep up with the demands of my work and home life.

- I find it very hard to relax or take it easy.

- It's hard for me to understand what people want from me.

- Anxiety about work or school is causing me a lot of stress.

- I often get stressed out because I'm afraid of getting fired or losing my job.

- I am bothered by the thought of failing at something.

- I often get stressed out because of unreasonable demands on my time or the behavior by others.

- Under pressure, I can't perform at my best.

- When things are tough, I stop trying and give up on myself and others.

- I often get stressed out because of my problems with others.

- It's hard for me to handle my own anger and get it under control.

- It's hard for me to get away from work and relax.

- I am not as confident as I would like to be.

- I have a hard time relaxing when things go wrong in my life or in the lives of those around me.

- Tomorrow, I'm likely to have too much to do.

- I often feel that nobody sees how hard it is for me just to get by in life.

- I often feel that others are not supportive of the things I do.

- It's hard for me to focus my attention on the things I need to do.

- My feelings are sometimes so intense they don't let me think rationally.

- It's hard for people to understand what I am thinking or feeling.

- When I try to calm myself down, I don't know how to do it.

- My relationships are often too stressful for me.

- I often have trouble finding the time to relax and rest.

- It's hard for me to get things done in a timely manner.

- I often feel overwhelmed by the pressures of work and family life.

- I often have trouble getting my work done.

These are just a few of the things that can cause chronic stress in ADHD individuals. A component of the emotional stress experienced by ADHD individuals is a lack of insight into their own emotional reactions.

Chronic Stress and Intrusion

There are a few common psychological triggers for chronic stress in people with ADHD:

- You feel unable to cope, so you shut down and withdraw from life temporarily.

- You worry that you're going to fail or that something terrible will happen.

- You worry so much about the things you don't have that you can't enjoy what you do have.

- All your problems seem to pile up and overwhelm you.

- You keep going on and on, trying to do too many things at once.

- When others make demands of you, it feels as if they are suffocating or smothering you.

- You feel as though others don't understand how difficult it is for you to do what they ask.

- You feel that you're misunderstood, and that people just don't know who you really are or how hard it is for you to get by in life.

- You feel so strongly about things and can't let go of your worries and concerns.

- You feel as though you don't have as much as others.

- The problems seem to be piling up in your life.

- If others continue to push, prod or criticize you, it can really stress you out.

- Having to get things done in a hurry can be stressful.

- If others around you are angry or frustrated, it can be stressful for you.

- You feel as though you are not getting the love and support you need from others.

- Your worry and fear can become so intense, you feel like there is no way out and everything is slipping away from you.

- You frequently agonize over mistakes or imagined mistakes.

- You often lose your temper or blow up at others who have hurt you.

- You often have trouble dealing with low self-esteem and feeling rejected by others.

- You feel powerless over your life.

- Your low self-esteem leads to very strong emotions that you are unable to calm down, so you shut off your emotions.

- You feel that you're letting others down or that others are disappointed in you.

- When things go wrong, you feel that it's your fault, even if it isn't your fault at all.

- Others continue to tell you "You're not good enough."

- You have trouble doing what others ask of you.

How to Overcome Chronic Stress

If you're experiencing chronic stress in your life, the first step is to acknowledge that it does exist. You may even need to seek help in order to do this. The next step is to address the things in your life that are causing the stress.

Chronic stress can be relieved by developing coping skills. Coping strategies include:

Awareness

Without awareness of what's causing you stress, it will be very difficult to over-come it. Recognizing the things in your life that make you stressed may improve your coping strategies. For example, if you feel trapped and helpless thinking about the future and don't like thoughts of failure and rejection, you might write down all your thoughts and feelings about events or situations that make you feel this way. You could then decide what situation or event is causing these feelings in the first place, then change it from a source of stress into a solution to a problem. If you are prone to feeling helpless or trapped by fear, instead of letting this fear paralyze you, write down everything that may traumatize you. By recognizing the things that are making you feel challenged and overwhelmed, you can see which situations need to be changed for your own benefit. For example, you might decide that it is okay to make mistakes because everyone does, or if things go wrong it means that God has a plan for your life after all.

It is also helpful to view the things in your life that are causing you stress as challenges, not threats. Then you can understand that the cause of your stress may be a good thing, because it provides you with an opportunity to grow or learn. You may be able to use these challenges as stepping stones to become better at coping with life.

Acceptance

It is necessary to accept the things in your life that are causing you stress. It is important to try not to let stress get in the way of who you are. It is also important not to let others' criticism or anger cause you any more stress. You can learn how to handle stressful situations by learning what you can do, when it is appropriate for you to be passive and when it is appropriate for you to control your reactions. For example, if someone says, "I don't know why you can't get anything done," it is important to learn how to keep your anger in check.

Acceptance does not mean that you just accept everything in your life. It is about managing your emotions instead of letting them cause you unnecessary stress. People with chronic stress often become stuck emotionally in unpleasant or difficult situations that they can't change for various reasons. You can learn to control your emotions by finding ways to be proactive and better at coping.

Develop stress-management and coping skills

Once you have identified what is causing you stress, you can develop new skills to manage it. This may mean learning how to build your self-esteem and how to deal with problems more effectively. You can learn about problem solving by asking yourself "What can I do?" instead of losing sleep wondering "What if things go wrong?" It is important to figure out what your resources are in any given situation. You can improve your ability to cope with stress by growing your awareness and acceptance of the situation as well as developing coping skills.

Reach out for help

It is important to learn how to ask for and receive help from others. This will not only give you a healthy balance in your life, it will also support and strengthen you. Don't be afraid that you aren't good enough or that what you want won't happen if you seek help from others, because people who have been through similar difficulties can provide crucial support.

Reaching out for help will also make you feel good about yourself and it can strengthen your ability to cope with life's stresses. Being able to seek help and accept the help that you do receive will help you to become a much stronger and more stable person.

Establish healthy boundaries between work and home

Stress is often the result of problems such as not getting enough done at work or home. Establishing healthy boundaries between work and home can break this cycle of stress.

For example, if you feel anxious or stressed about something that happened at work, talk to a friend or a co-worker about your problems instead of going home and discussing them with your spouse or family members. It is also important not to consider the problems at work as your personal failure. It is helpful to keep these problems separate from your home life, because it helps avoid bringing your stress home with you.

Find healthy coping strategies

Any stress can become chronic if it is not dealt with properly. Find some healthy coping strategies to help you deal with difficult situations in a better way. These strategies can help reduce stress and make you feel more in control of your life.

Dealing With Your Home Life and Financial Responsibilities

It's common for adults with ADHD to have a hard time staying on top of their financial responsibilities. This is why it is very necessary to have a budget and recognize where your money goes. If you realize there are areas in which you are spending more than necessary, try making adjustments. One of the most important keys to managing your money is to know what you are spending. Once you know what you are paying for, you can determine whether or not it is a necessary expense. If it doesn't make sense to spend the money, don't spend it. Another way to handle your finances is to make a list of things you need to buy and prioritize them. This can help you see the bigger picture and figure out how to balance your money.

Once you know the essentials, look at each item on your list, determine if it is something you truly want or need and whether it fits in with your priorities. If not, toss the idea out. If it does, make sure there is enough money in the budget for the item. If there isn't, put the item on hold until there is. If you see you are spending more than what is necessary in a particular area, make changes to get yourself back on track. If you can't afford what you need, look at ways in which you can make adjustments to get by with what you've got. If there are things you don't need, make the decision to eliminate them from your life. You could also find a way to earn some extra money on the side. This can help put extra cash in your pocket, save more money, and feel more accomplished.

People with ADHD also tend to have challenges maintaining an orderly home environment. Sometimes, this is simply because ADHD can make it hard to organize things. But, at the same time, people with ADHD often have very active imaginations, which can give rise to clutter.

Sometimes, people with ADHD are also too impatient to finish certain household tasks or don't want to do them at all.

To overcome these challenges, you must learn to organize. It can be really helpful to start with a single room. This way, you don't have to worry about the other stuff in the house. It's important to get organized for your own sanity, and because it will make your life easier.

You can also be creative with your organization. Use a color-coded system to keep track of things. You can also organize your home by storing the things you need the most frequently in one place so you don't always have to go hunting for them. And if something takes up too much room, such as a big TV set, it may be helpful to store it in another room or move it into storage until you need it again. As you learn more about ways to better organize your home, you will improve the way you manage your household.

If it's hard for you to stay organized with all the things happening in your brain, it may be useful to use some kind of system or tool that will keep track of what you are doing and give you reminders. This can help you stay on task and make your life more orderly.

Get a weekly or monthly planner that will remind you to take out the garbage, water plants, etc. You could also use an "organized closet" to organize what items you may want to get rid of and what you will need in the future. Just take any items or clothes you don't use or need and put them in a box and find places to put the boxes so they won't clutter your house.

If organization is still an issue, make time for yourself each day, week, month to clean up your place to make it more manageable.

I know this may seem like a lot of work, but it will make a big difference in your life. People with ADHD find that the more organized their home is, the more organized they are in their lives. Organizing your home could be one of the keys to keeping yourself orderly and on top of things at home as well as outside of it.

Other Disorders Adults with ADHD Can Experience

Adults with ADHD are at greater risk for several other psychiatric disorders, including:

• *Anxiety*

Adults with ADHD are at greater risk of having an anxiety disorder or panic attack because they are more sensitive to stress. Some symptoms of ADHD are also the same as those of anxiety, so it can be very difficult to tell the difference. Adults with both disorders experience excessive worry, fear, and tension. Similar to ADHD, adults with anxiety tend to have a problem with concentration, attention, and impulse control.

• *Depression*

Adults with ADHD may be prone to depression, a mental health disorder that causes an extreme sadness and loss of interest in things that used to be enjoyable. Depression is also characterized by a lack of energy and motivation rather than hyperactivity. Adults with ADHD and depression may also experience symptoms such as agitated body movements, insomnia, difficulty concentrating, and difficulty feeling pleasure. The depression symptoms sometimes vary from mild to severe; some adults may require medication or therapy to help treat their symptoms.

• Problems with alcohol and drugs

Adults with ADHD may use alcohol and drugs to self-medicate their symptoms. If they did not receive proper treatment for their disorder in childhood, they may have learned that drugs and alcohol can help them cope with the problems they face in adulthood. However, problems with these substances can cause serious health problems for adults, including impaired memory and learning abilities. Adults who use drugs or alcohol regularly may be at higher risk of chronic disorders such as depression and drug addiction.

• Bipolar Disorder

Adults with ADHD are also at higher risk of bipolar disorder, which causes extreme mood swings. Adults with bipolar disorder can go from being extremely happy or angry to being sad or depressed, seemingly without any provocation from the outside world. In some cases, a manic episode can be characterized by symptoms of ADHD such as hyperactivity and impulsivity.

• Eating disorders

Adults with ADHD are at higher risk of binge eating and purging. A binge-eating episode occurs when a person eats a large amount of food in an uncomfortably short time period. In purging disorders, food is thrown up in order to get rid of the calories consumed during the binge. Many adults with ADHD have difficulty controlling their emotions. They may think that because they are unable to control the impulse to eat the cookies or sweets they crave, their emotions must also be uncontrollable. In response to these emotions, they may feel that vomiting, laxatives, or other unhealthy behaviors will help to ease the way they feel.

• Phobias

Adults with ADHD may also be more likely to have a phobia, which is a persistent and unreasonable fear of a specified object or situation. Some of the most common phobias among adults include fear of spiders, snakes, heights, and public speaking. While these fears are considered normal for children, they are considered signs of an abnormality for adults.

• Obsessive-Compulsive Disorder

Adults with ADHD are more likely to have obsessive-compulsive disorder, the main symptom of which is uncontrollable thoughts. Other symptoms include repetitive behaviors to meet certain mental demands and an inability to control actions without experiencing discomfort. Adults with OCD are likely to be preoccupied with cleanliness or thoughts about having to organize everything.

• Sleep disorders

Adults with ADHD are at risk of sleep disorders including sleep apnea, insomnia, and restless leg syndrome. Sleep apnea is a condition characterized by the collapse of the throat during sleep, which causes breathing to stop or become shallow. Sleep apnea can be caused by excess weight, hormonal imbalances, or certain medical conditions. Insomnia is a disorder that causes difficulty falling asleep, a lack of quality of sleep, and waking up too early in the morning. Restless leg syndrome is a condition characterized by an uncontrollable urge to move the legs while lying down. These disorders can cause fatigue and poor concentration.

• Impulsivity

Adults with ADHD are more likely to develop an addiction to gambling or compulsive shopping. Those who struggle with impulse control may get so caught up in the physical act of shopping that they do not know when to stop. Compulsive gambling can be caused by exposure to visually stimulating images, excitement, and other people's actions at the casino or racetrack. Those who experience these compulsions may keep gambling, despite their growing losses.

• Schizophrenia

Adults with ADHD are also more likely to develop schizophrenia. This disorder is characterized by hallucinations that cannot be explained by external stimuli or any other medical condition, as well as delusions that cause the affected person to behave irrationally. People with schizophrenia may also feel detached from reality and from others around them, and they often experience difficulty concentrating. Adults with ADHD are at risk of developing schizophrenia because they are more likely to have symptoms of impulsivity, difficulty controlling their emotions, and mood instability. Schizophrenia can cause many problems in daily functioning, including social isolation and poor work performance.

CHAPTER 13: DIET AND PHYSICAL ACTIVITY TO ENHANCE FOCUS AND MANAGE EMOTIONS

The Best Treatments for Adult ADHD

If you're looking for treatments for adult ADHD, there are many different options out there. Some of the most popular alternatives include therapy, exercise, diet changes, medication, and music therapy. It's really important to find what works best for you.

Therapy has been shown to be effective in treating ADHD symptoms. Counseling can help patients identify negative thoughts and behaviors that contribute to their symptoms and teach strategies of coping with these problems more effectively. Such techniques also help in improving interpersonal skills, promoting positive emotions, and bringing out a patient's purpose in life.

Although there are no drugs that are specifically indicated for the treatment of adult ADHD, there are several medications you may nonetheless be prescribed. You may be able to take medication without a problem if you don't drink alcohol or use other drugs. As with any medication, you should not take it if you're pregnant or breastfeeding. You should also tell your doctor if you have a history of drug abuse, heart disease, high blood pressure, glaucoma, liver disease, and breathing problems such as asthma.

Aside from therapy and medication, exercise is a popular alternative treatment for ADHD. Studies have also shown that exercise can improve symptoms of ADHD in adults. A study in 2005 published in the *Archives of Internal Medicine*, for example, found that a moderate exercise routine improved attention and behavior in patients with ADHD. Researchers assigned 43 overweight or obese middle-aged men with ADHD to either an aerobic exercise program or a stretching and toning program for 12 weeks. After 12 weeks, the exercise group showed an improved ability to pay attention, follow directions, control impulses, and regulate emotions.

A study from the *Journal of Attention Disorders* found that aerobic exercise can also improve symptoms of ADHD in some children. Researchers recruited 54 boys with ADHD to participate in either an 80-minute outdoor program that included physical activity or 80-minutes of traditional aquatic programs. After 10 weeks, children who participated in outdoor exercise experienced significant improvement in attention, emotional control, and overall symptoms.

The benefits of exercise are also seen long-term for adult ADHD patients. A 2005 study published in the *Journal of Attention Disorders* found that the effects of exercise on ADHD symptoms can last up to six months after participating in a regular fitness program. Researchers studied 37 children and adolescents with ADHD and 35 people without ADHD who participated in a physical activity program. After six months, both groups maintained their improved attention and organization skills.

The right diet can also help manage adult ADHD symptoms. Researchers studied the diets of 61 adults with an ADHD diagnosis. The subjects were grouped into two: one group was given a Mediterranean diet and the other group was given a standard American diet. After three months, those who followed the

Mediterranean diet experienced significantly lower levels of hyperactivity and impulsivity.

Exercise and diet, however, do not remove all symptoms of adult ADHD. In these cases, people with ADHD can try music therapy as a method of treatment. Music therapy helps improve attention and focus by reducing over-stimulation and negative reactions.

During a session, a therapist may ask you to pick a piece of music that makes you feel happy or sad. You then learn how to use this music as an emotional tool to help manage your feelings and behavior. Since music therapy does not use medication, it's a good alternative for those who can't take any form of drugs. It's also a great option for those who desire to use alternative therapies.

ADHD can be difficult to overcome. Finding the right treatment method may help alleviate some of the symptoms of adult ADHD.

Eating Healthy

Be sure to eat healthy meals on a regular basis. There are some foods that increase your blood sugar levels and cause you to become more impulsive. Processed foods and junk foods typically cause the most problems for people with ADHD.

Many people with ADHD often do not eat very healthily because they are not able to focus on the importance of eating right. They may also be more inclined to skip meals because of their busy schedules or because they are distracted.

If you have ADHD, try to make sure you are eating a balanced diet. Make sure your meals contain a lot of proteins, fruits and vegetables. Try to eat healthy snacks throughout the day.

People with ADHD often tend to become hungry throughout the day. This can be a sign that you are not getting enough nutrients and it is time to start taking some supplements. Getting the right supplements will likely help you manage your ADHD and will allow you to get better results from your treatment.

Nutrition Action Steps

Your diet has to do with how you feel on a daily basis. If you want to get better results from your ADHD treatment, make sure that your diet is in check. Try eating more proteins and healthy fats in your everyday meals. This can be an effective way to manage your hunger.

Eliminate or decrease caffeine and alcohol consumption. Both these substances can cause you to become more focused on the world around you and make it harder for you to focus on yourself. Cut back or eliminate them completely.

Add some cold-water fish or fish oil supplements to your everyday routine. Both of these are known for helping with ADHD.

The Power of Sleep

People with ADHD can benefit from getting more sleep each night. Although it may seem difficult to get enough sleep at first, it can be very rewarding in the long run.

Restful, restorative sleep is a very powerful tool for regulating mood and maintaining attention throughout your day. If you are not getting enough sleep each night, you are likely to experience some negative consequences.

Going to bed on time every day is a habit that can do wonders for your body and mind. Try creating a routine that helps your body prepare for the next day of activities. When you wake up, try to get started with your morning activities immediately so you become more productive throughout the day.

CHAPTER 14: CONQUERING ADHD CHALLENGES

Eventually, you'll reach a point where you are ready to make a break from the past. Your adult life may be full of good memories and accomplishments, but it's become clear that your childhood struggles need to end. You're no longer that little person who needs help packing his backpack or crossing the street. You've got this!

That being said, just because ADHD isn't stopping you anymore doesn't mean it doesn't still exist. It is important to stay on top of your medications or other treatment options.

ADHD often manifests in different ways as we mature. Many adults with ADHD say that the main thing they struggle with is being unable to focus on certain things that need to be done, or putting too much emphasis on one task over another.

For example, I have a hard time watching TV commercials. They can either be too long or too short, and I lose interest quickly.

Paying attention to what your co-workers are doing can be challenging. You may find yourself drifting off and missing important details. I'm lucky that my boss is understanding and understands that this isn't a lack of attention, but rather a symptom of my ADHD.

ADHD is probably the hardest thing to deal with in your adult life. Don't let this discourage you. People who struggle with ADHD are more than capable of achieving whatever is thrown at them… they just need to learn the right strategies.

What to Do When the World Gets in Your Way

When you have issues with your ADHD, the first thing you want to do is take a look at your environment. Are there things in your home that make you uncomfortable, or do things seem a bit off? This could be asthma causing you to cough more often, or a noise from your neighbor that makes it hard for you to focus. The next step is eliminating those "off" things from the environment as much as possible.

You should also get rid of possessions that are causing you stress. One of my relatives got rid of his obsessive-compulsive disorder by selling all the stuff he didn't use anymore. He found that his room felt lighter, and he was able to breathe easier.

You should also get rid of things that aren't helping you in the long run. Things like magazines with pictures of pretty models or lots of ads for junk food can be distracting and can lead you to buy more things than you need.

Also, get rid of overused items around your house. If you have one chair in your house, and it's used every day, it may be time to upgrade your furniture.

However, do not to get rid of all your old stuff. Many people with ADHD need to take a break from their lives to process the memories and value the things they hold close. Choose some of your old things and label them for safekeeping. This way, you can remember the good times and what was important to you once upon a time.

Developing Self-Discipline and Willpower

You may find that ADHD has led you to develop a bad habit or two. When you were young, your habits weren't so important, and what you did didn't matter. But now that you're older, it's time to get honest with yourself and recognize your habits during their infancy before they begin to play a bigger role in your life.

Don't expect yourself to change overnight, but rather work on developing the willpower you need to change for the better. There are so many ways to do this, but the two most important things are to sit down and then make a plan, and to exercise discipline.

If you want to learn how to kick a bad habit, then try the following:

1. Make a visual representation of your bad habit – Before you start, make a picture of your bad habit so you have something to look at during the process.

2. Record your thoughts – Double check to make sure this is what you really want. You may "want" to eat a lot of junk food, but if you think about all the money wasted on those snacks and those sweets, then those thoughts will surely inspire some willpower.

3. Break your bad habit into chunks – You don't have to change everything overnight, so take it in steps.

4. Think about what you're gaining by making the change – If you're feeling hungry after exercising, think about all the money you'll save on certain food items. If you want to stop eating junk food, concentrate on all of the benefits that will come with your new healthy lifestyle.

5. Always be honest with yourself – Are you really ready to change, or are you just saying that because everyone else is doing it?

6. Work on group projects –It can be a great motivator to join forces with others.

"It takes the most disciplined people not to do something." – Dr. Seuss

Learning how to control your impulse control is an area that is both simple and powerful. Whenever you feel an impulse coming on, stop and think about your actions. You need to have discipline if you want to get out of the rut that is ADHD.

Corresponding Impulses with Appropriate Actions

When your impulses are getting the best of you, it's important to develop a way for your actions to match your impulses. If you're having a hard time stopping yourself from eating, you'll have to find a way to keep food out of your sight and away from your hands.

You should also find a way to mentally put yourself in place of those things that come up as triggers. Just as you know what makes you angry or anxious, so should you be able to identify how those emotions can trigger an impulse. If they don't, it's likely they will become too strong and cause some disastrous actions.

Don't overthink this. Just let the impulses flow and follow the thoughts as they come.

I know this is difficult for those with ADHD, but it's important that you recognize the triggers that can affect you and then develop a plan of action. You can't just sit around and expect things to change on their own. Once you're ready, learn how to control your impulses and turn those energies into something positive.

Accepting the Present and Making the Best of Your Situation

Many things can be accomplished if you take a minute to look at your situation and accept it for what it is. Too often we look at the negatives that surround us and interpret them as such.

If you're ADHD, then you have to accept that things will go wrong from time to time. It's not easy to change, but it's necessary if you want a better outlook on life. Learn to make the best of what you have now.

"We cannot save the world by being aware of our suffering." – Karen Honeycutt

You're going to experience good days and bad days. There will be moments when it feels like you just won't get anything done, but eventually that will pass and you'll feel your energy coming back. That's just how living is.

It's okay to feel a little down every now and then, but don't let it affect you long term. It's really important that you stay positive and focus on what you can do to make your situation better.

Don't be afraid of these times. Instead, use them as feedback that you need to make changes in your life.

CHAPTER 15: ESSENTIAL KNOWLEDGE TO OVERCOME ADHD

The adult with ADHD has a lot of challenges in their life, but is this a bad thing? In the long run, ADHD can be considered a positive thing because it gives you the chance to work on yourself and overcome your problems.

Here's an important list of things you should think about if you have ADHD:

1. Don't give up on yourself

Maybe in the past you've given up when things got hard, but don't do that now. It's not going to do anything except ruin your self-esteem. You can't let these failures stop you from doing something great.

2. Let go of mistakes

This is a hard one for those with ADHD because we tend to take everything on our shoulders. Remember that no one is perfect. People make mistakes all the time, so learn how to let it go and move on.

3. Learn to fight your impulses

This is something that you'll likely deal with if you have ADHD. It's important to learn how to battle yourself so that you can do what needs to be done. It's just like fighting an opposing army, but with your own thoughts and actions coming at you from all angles.

4. Accept your feelings

Not every minute of the day is going to be happy and full of joy. That's just how life is. Focus on all those different emotions and understand how they affect your actions. If you notice that you're feeling down, then try to learn why and use those moments as feedback for yourself.

5. Make the right friends

There will be those around you who support what you're doing and those who don't understand or care about it at all. You'll have to learn which is which and choose your friends accordingly. This isn't something that will happen overnight, but you should try to make some friends who are understanding.

6. Try to understand yourself

When you understand yourself, you'll be able to identify what parts of your personality need improvement and then target them for action. It's so important that you believe in yourself and try to calm your negative impulses whenever they occur.

7. Let yourself be who you are

You can't understand others if you don't understand yourself. The reason why people get along with one another is because they know how to accept each other for who they are. If you make an attempt to focus on your strengths, then it's easier to rid yourself of the parts you'd like to change.

8. Acknowledge your positive qualities

This is something that those with ADHD often forget to do it. It's so simple to focus on the negative qualities and completely ignore the positive ones. Instead, look at all your positive qualities and focus on them as much as you can.

9. Don't underestimate yourself

This is something that many adults with ADHD have a habit of doing. It's understandable, but you shouldn't underestimate yourself. You have a lot of knowledge that will help others and it's your responsibility to share your knowledge with them.

10. Don't focus on punishment

When you punish yourself, it's never the thing that works. Instead, look at the lessons that you learn and how you can use this to help others.

11. Learn to forgive yourself

This is something that many people struggle with when they have ADHD or when they're in an abusive relationship like many adults with ADHD are in. You must learn how to forgive yourself so that you can be a better person.

12. Learn from your mistakes

One of the best ways to figure out what you need to change is by learning from your mistakes. Find those moments where it went wrong and then think about what you could have done differently. This will help your future actions and allow those around you to see a better side of you.

13. Find the fun

This is something that those with ADHD often have a problem with. Learn how to have fun and let loose as this will help you relax and take some pressure off of yourself.

14. Know when to ask for help

It doesn't matter how smart or strong you are, sometimes you'll need help. You can't do all things by yourself, so don't pretend that you can. Look for someone who can help with what you're struggling with and ask them for guidance when needed.

15. Take care of your body

When you have ADHD, it's very important to eat healthy foods, move around enough, and get enough sleep. If necessary, find someone who can help you with this and teach you how to take care of yourself.

16. Accept that you can be happy

You can be happy when you understand who you are and what you need to do in order to live a better life. It's important that you don't just wallow in your misery. Instead, learn how to enjoy the things around you.

17. Explode with passion

If you have ADHD, it often means you're passionate about the things you do. Don't let this passion fizzle out because it can help lead you to greatness. Find people who share your passions and do something amazing together.

18. Make your goals realistic

Everyone wants to reach greatness. Those with ADHD, however, may have a tendency to overreach. This can lead to disappointment down the road. Instead, try setting realistic goals that are easier to achieve.

19. Know when to stop

There are times when it's best not to keep pushing. Know when to stop and try something new. Learn how to change your actions and find something that works instead of continually doing the same thing over and over again.

20. Be grateful

If you're living with ADHD, be grateful that you're still alive and can do great things with your life. Instead of focusing on the negatives, be happy for what you do have.

How to Not Get Attacked by Others

There are many reasons why people might attack you. Sometimes it's because of your behavior or attitude, and sometimes it's just because of their own issues. The best way to avoid getting attacked by others is to simply not give them a reason to do so in the first place. Here are some tips for doing that:

Your behavior should be calm and pleasant. That means no shouting, screaming, hitting, threatening, flip-out rages, psychotic sermons, or otherwise inappropriate behavior. This is particularly true in public places where you might upset or scare people. There's a difference between being angry and being psychotic. If you're angry because of something someone did to you, ask yourself if it's really worth blowing up over. If it is, cool down until you can deal with the situation in a calm way. If it's not, think about changing your perspective. It's probably not as important to you as you think it is. Once you've taken a step back from the situation, see what conclusions you can draw from the problem and how the people involved might have behaved better. How can you make things better? If the person who hurt you apologized, asked for your forgiveness or promised to change his or her behavior, it's not really worth continuing to fight with them.

Don't take things personally. One of the greatest ways to avoid conflicts with others is to not take things personally. It is important to realize that other people's actions are often not about you. They are usually about themselves, their problems, and their issues. So before you take things personally or feel hurt by someone, look at their actions in the context of everything else they do in life, and try to give them the benefit of the doubt.

Don't give other people the opportunity to attack you. There are many things people do that may offend, annoy, or anger other people. Avoid these things so you don't give people a reason to attack you. For example, if you know that someone is easily offended by certain things, then don't say those things around them.

Don't take advantage of others. Taking advantage of other people can cause them to feel resentment and anger towards you. Be sure to give everyone equal opportunities and treatment.

Take the high road. When you do this, many people will see your behavior as an act of kindness and generosity towards them. Always be generous, good-natured, and kind to everyone around you.

When people show respect towards you, it is important to show them equal respect in return. Not doing so can cause others to feel contempt for you, which can lead to an attack.

Ignore people who try to attack you. If someone does try to attack you in some way, the best thing you can do is just ignore them. Often, people attack you because they think it will make them feel better. But if you ignore them, they won't get the satisfaction they were looking for and will usually stop trying.

Avoid complaining. Complaining can be one of the easiest ways to get under people's skin. If you constantly complain about other people, especially in front of them, it can easily raise their anger levels to the point where they lash out at you. Sometimes it's not the content of what you are saying, but how often you are saying it. For example, if your job is annoying you by giving you too much work, you might have a legitimate gripe. But if you complain about this to everyone you know all day, every day, it can wear people out. It's very important to be aware of how much complaining you are doing. Pay attention to the number of times you complain each day. Remember that even if your complaint is legitimate, it's best not to let everyone around you know about it.

Manage your emotions. When someone makes a comment about your behavior it is better to stand your ground and not react than to fall into the trap of becoming defensive or argumentative. It does no good for anyone if you are yelling at the top of your lungs.

Learn to use your words. It is very common for people with ADHD to be misunderstood by others. Sometimes it can seem like you are talking too much or not responding when in reality you are listening intently and processing information, albeit at a different pace to other members of the conversation. Learning to express yourself calmly and concisely will help reduce the likelihood that someone will misinterpret you as being rude or argumentative.

If a person is pressuring you to do something or you feel like you might explode, it can be helpful to take a time out and give yourself a few minutes away from the situation. Just tell the person that you need a break and some time alone so you can calm down. When you feel like yourself again, come back and approach the situation more calmly.

How to Heal Yourself When Other People Attack You

What do you do when someone has hurt you? What do you do when they have attacked you or challenged your self-image? How do you cope with the agony of rejection, snubs, insults, or loneliness?

The first thing to remember is that you are not alone. Everyone has felt this way at one time or another. Nobody has the right to judge your feelings. The second thing to be reminded is that these painful events happen for a reason. They happen because they are supposed to happen. They are not random events. They are part of the process of life. You can learn something about yourself by observing your reactions. As you go through this process, you will begin to understand how what has happened to you has actually created something good for you in the long run. It is important that when someone attacks you, you do not just think of yourself but what others will think or feel about it too. You need to be mindful, compassionate, and understanding because when someone attacks you there is often a lot of pain behind it.

Recognizing the pain and the hurt it causes is the first step to healing. Recognizing this pain will help you heal as well as give you a sense of closure. It is important that you do not just let the pain bleed into your life and ruin your day or week. You also need to be mindful that some people will inflict more damage than others. Some people don't even realize they hurt you and will continue on with their lives without apologizing or showing any remorse for what they have done. This is when you need to recognize the importance of letting go of it. You cannot be upset with someone forever. You cannot carry someone else's burden of guilt and self-hatred forever. At some point, you need to take control back and let go. With time, people learn how to deal with new situations and let go of the negative emotions that surround them. You should have a little bit of patience and wait for that time to come, because it will come eventually.

Another way to deal with the pain is to be in a positive mood. You can listen to your favorite music or go for a walk, exercise, do yoga, meditate, paint pictures in watercolor or buy yourself a pretty picture. The main objective of doing these activities is to bring you into a positive mood and keep your mind off the person who hurt you. Being in a good mood will help you heal faster because when you are in a good mood, your mind is more open and receptive which helps in healing. Being in a more positive mood also helps you feel better about yourself and the world around you. Also, when you are in a more positive mood, it is easier to come up with ways to deal with the situation, and heal from the pain.

Another way of dealing with the pain of rejection is by spending time alone or taking time for yourself. You could either walk outside or take a bath to clear your mind of all the negativity surrounding you. You can try to acquire a new skill or just do something to occupy your time. Do whatever it takes to bring you into a good mood again, since having a bad mood will only make it harder for you to heal from the pain.

When your mood has improved, you should be able to regain control of yourself and your faith in those around you. Go back to the person who hurt you and talk with him or her about it. You can tell them that you are sad about what they said to you and that it makes you feel bad. Do not expect the other person to apologize to you, or you are just going to go through the same pain again.

After you have talked with the person, you are probably going to feel better in time. You may move on with your life. You are not a bad person because of what happened. Remember that you are not the only individual who feels this way. It is okay to be sad about it but there is no reason for you to be alone in your sadness when there are so many people out there who care about you, who love you, and who will take care of you, no matter what happens.

CHAPTER 16: GETTING THE RIGHT HELP AND SUPPORT

Many adults with ADHD are dealing with symptoms every day, but don't receive the help they need. They may even be unaware that they have the disorder. It is common for adults struggling with self-care, low self-esteem, and relationships to not realize that there is a medical reason behind their difficulties. Adults who suffer from ADHD should be able to reach out for help from those around them as well as from mental health professionals.

In addition to professional help, reading books about ADHD can provide a good starting point for understanding this disorder and its effects on adult life. A book can help you learn about ADHD, as well as provide some basic insight into the disorder. A book can also help you find the information you need to help you overcome your difficulties in daily life. It can also provide support and understanding from someone who has "been there." Reading is a good way to learn about ADHD and improve your life.

Increasing Your Knowledge about ADHD

Many people with ADHD feel that what really matters is their ability to function in life. They may believe that the only important thing is to get a good job and become successful in life. If this fails, they may even attempt suicide. However, many people with ADHD have no idea why they are struggling. They think it is because of their failure to do something correctly, or because they did not work hard enough, or because other people did not support them. They may find it difficult to understand that, in reality, they are dealing with serious limitations that are greatly impacting their ability to function in life.

As is true for many psychiatric disorders, the more time you spend researching the disorder and understanding it better through books, experts' opinions, or experiences with others, the better prepared you will be to handle the challenges that ADHD presents.

If you are struggling with ADHD, you may not understand why you are facing the problems you are. You may feel like ADHD is an obstacle that you can't overcome. You may feel like your brain is not working right, or that you are being punished for something that wasn't your fault. You may also feel that your family just does not understand this disorder. If any of these things ring true for you, it means that now is the time to step back and learn more about ADHD. By learning more, you can take action to start treating your ADHD symptoms. You may even discover that your symptoms are likely to get worse as time goes on. If this is the case, now is the time to start taking action.

There are different ways you can acquire knowledge about ADHD. You can find out more about the disorder on the Internet, talk to your doctors and mental health professionals, or volunteer at a local organization for adults with ADHD. There are also many excellent online educational resources that are free for the taking but are very helpful to those who struggle with this disorder.

Take the time to read and learn as much as you can. The more you know, the better equipped you will be to cope with ADHD and improve your life.

You might also want to talk to other people who have ADHD. Discussing your difficulties can help you understand how others cope. You can also learn about treatment options and how to cope on your own.

You might also consider joining an online or in-person support group. These groups can be great resources for meeting others who are dealing with the same issues you are facing, as well as providing the knowledge and support needed to improve your life.

Taking online classes can be another very helpful way to learn about ADHD and its symptoms. Online courses offer an opportunity to receive information from expert educators, as well as record your responses and progress. Online classes can provide you with a friendly forum where you can interact with other students who have the same symptoms that you have. They can help give you a broad perspective on ADHD, as well as provide some insight into treatments and resources available.

Now that you have this understanding, you can begin to take action. You may also discover that there is no simple cure for ADHD; rather, there are many things you can do to minimize the impact it has on your life.

Giving Yourself the Best Chance with Self-Help

Some people with ADHD may struggle with feeling alone. You might feel as though no one really understands what you're going through.

There will always be those who know what you're going through and those who don't. It's important that you don't get angry with others when they don't understand what you've been through. This is life and sometimes people won't see things from your point of view.

If you take away one thing from this book, let it be that ADHD isn't something to be afraid of or ashamed of. It has advantages and also disadvantages, just like any other characteristic of human beings. Don't let your fear of judgment hold you back from doing what you want to do.

Don't let another person's actions determine how you feel about yourself. This is life and it's okay to be angry. Hate the situation, but never hate others. Learn from their actions and don't let it bother you because your anger won't help anyone.

There will be many things you can't change, but it's important that you start thinking about the things you can. Focus on the things you can control and do not let other people determine your actions. Focus on yourself and what matters to your future.

There's no reason for you to feel sad just because someone else doesn't understand what you've been through and who you are. Life is too short and it doesn't matter what others think. Keep moving forward no matter what.

If you're ever feeling depressed or alone, then seek help. Accept the reality of the situation and realize that there are people who care about you.

If you have problems with substance use or addiction, understand that there are support groups for these things. If you're thinking about hurting yourself or another person, seek help right away. You can't do anything to change what happened in the past, but you can always control what you do from now on.

Alternative and Complementary Treatment for ADHD

ADHD symptoms can be destructive. Doctors and pharmacists often prescribe medication for ADHD treatment which can be very effective but may come with side effects. While medication is a great way to reduce symptoms, alternative and complementary treatments may also help to relieve symptoms and create more harmony in your life:

• *Relaxation Training*

This promotes the development of overall self-awareness and self-control in individuals seeking to reduce their symptoms or withdraw from medication. It teaches individuals to control their emotions, thoughts, and actions in order to become more effective in performing everyday tasks. The program teaches the individual about the connection between emotions, body tension, breathing patterns, and physical health. It also delves into how negative thinking affects energy flow through the body. The techniques involved in this type of treatment are similar to those used in meditation.

• *Mindfulness*

The practice of mindfulness has become very popular because it helps individuals manage their attention and emotional responses. People who suffer from ADHD may have difficulty paying attention, sitting still, and focusing on the task at hand. Mindfulness is a way of being fully present in the moment. This can be accomplished by having an open awareness of thought, emotion, sensation, and the environment. It has been found that many adults with ADHD are impulsive because they are constantly seeking stimulation to distract themselves from boredom. ADHD is characterized by distractibility or mind wandering. Mindfulness gives people with ADHD a new perspective on life. It helps them to gain focus and become more aware of their surroundings.

• *Neurofeedback*

This is a treatment for ADHD in which electrodes are placed on the head to monitor brain waves and provide feedback to patients about their levels of attention and relaxation. The electrodes usually pick up the electromagnetic waves emitted by cells in the brain when neurons fire. The patient is then taught how to control these brain waves by using biofeedback training in order to modify their behavior. Brain wave training can be useful in treating ADHD because it allows the brain to focus more effectively on the task at hand. It is also able to block dysfunctional or excessive patterns of brain activity.

• *Neurotherapy*

This is another treatment strategy that focuses on the nervous system and how it works by altering factors such as stress, medication, diet, and sleep habits. Neurotherapy uses the techniques of biofeedback and neurofeedback to help an individual recognize his or her patterns of attention. This often leads to improved self-awareness and a greater sense of control. Neurotherapy can be more effective when combined with behavioral therapy.

• *Sound Therapy*

This treatment is used to produce a relaxing, meditative state by listening to specific sounds. A variety of sounds such as nature sounds, binaural beats, and meditation music can be programmed into an MP3 player and listened to at home or in the office during stressful or busy periods. The goal is to enhance attention and reduce stress levels.

• *Tai Chi*

This martial art is known to improve mood, enhance ability to concentrate, and improve overall well-being. It helps to increase energy and awareness and teaches the individual to relax the mind and body and live in the present moment. Its goal is to slow down the body and be more aware of our surroundings.

• *Yoga*

Yoga will help you deal with anxiety as well as anxiety attacks, and has been known to reduce the symptoms of ADHD.

• *Acupuncture*

This treatment is based on the Chinese theory that energy flows through 12 pathways in the body called meridians. When this energy is disrupted, illness occurs. Acupuncture helps to redirect and balance this energy flow and return it to normal. It works by stimulating specific points along these meridians with thin needles to adjust chemical levels in the brain and nervous system. It can reduce hyperactivity in children and adults with ADHD.

• *Meditation*

The practice of meditation involves the individual's ability to focus their attention on one thought, emotion, or sensation at a time. It is very important for individuals who suffer from ADHD to be able to concentrate and focus on something other than themselves because this can help them gain control over their actions and thoughts. Meditating is a creative way for people with ADHD to relax and regain focus.

• *Holistic Treatment*

This is a treatment that emphasizes the relationship between mind, body, and spirit. It helps individuals gain a better understanding of themselves in order to modify unwanted habits and behaviors. The objective of holistic treatment is to help a person learn how their emotional, physical, and mental states affect their life in a positive way. It teaches the individual to become more in control of his or her environment.

• *Psychotherapy*

Psychotherapy often involves working on the past and how you developed your personality. It teaches individuals how to identify and express their feelings and emotions in a healthy way. Psychotherapy can be helpful for treating ADHD by increasing awareness of the present moment and of the connections between thoughts, emotions, and actions.

CHAPTER 17: ASSISTING OTHERS IN MANAGING ADHD

Many people with ADHD have a very difficult time asking for help. They worry others will not take them seriously and that they might be seen as a burden. They often hesitate to reach out because they fear being rejected or even ridiculed.

Often it is hard for an adult with ADHD to ask for help, but there are some simple ways you can help them.

Writing a letter, email, or blog post can be a great way to motivate someone with ADHD. Stating how you or someone you know succeeded can help them believe they can do it too.

Being an active listener is also a way to help someone with ADHD overcome their challenges. Listen without telling them what to do or how to accomplish it. Let them figure out the best way to achieve their goal, then be there for support when they follow through.

Be patient. Don't hurry them, as this can lead to them getting frustrated. Remind them that you understand, and stay patient. Help them to look at the big picture. Ask them to focus on what they are accomplishing, instead of how long it is taking to accomplish it.

Don't judge them for taking longer to accomplish a task, or for not following through on something they said they'd do.

Make sure you are able to talk things over calmly. If you want the person with ADHD to be calm about the situation at hand, then you need to be calm as well. Put things in their perspective and tell them that you will be there to support them in the future.

It is important when you help someone with ADHD to try to understand the frustration they are going through when they are trying to accomplish something. When the person with ADHD is overly frustrated, help them by letting them know that you will be there for support.

Be aware of their needs. Give them space and time to accomplish what they set out to do. If they seem to be stuck on something, offer to get together and brainstorm. If they need a deadline or a reminder to get them going, try setting one.

Encourage them. When you are trying to help someone with ADHD, let them know how proud you are of them. Giving only criticism will only make them feel worse about themselves. Let them know that you are proud to have someone you can depend on.

Encouragement and Support

It is important to support and encourage people who have ADHD.

Many people with ADHD tend to misjudge other people's emotions. Some don't realize how important their friends and family are to them, nor do they acknowledge that those close to them care about them as much as they do.

People with ADHD may not always know how to express their love or concern. They may also not know what other people want them to do.

Try to make the other person feel secure and confident. Let them know that you are there for support. If they are having trouble achieving something, whether it's because of distractions or just due to their inability to process everything that is going on at once, try to help them. Remind them of their past achievements and give them a deadline to work towards.

Give them space and time to think about what they want to do. If they need help, let them know that you care and offer to get together and brainstorm about an idea. It is important not to keep pressuring them because it will only make things worse. It might even discourage them from trying again later on.

Encourage others with ADHD to see the big picture, so they recognize how far they have come. If they have trouble focusing, try to help them concentrate on the task at hand. It is important to give them short breaks, so they have time to digest everything you have told them.

If they still struggle, it may be best not to force them to do something they can't handle at the moment.

Emphasize their strengths and accomplishments in order to raise their self-esteem.

At times, ADHD does interfere with learning and communicating. But this doesn't mean that people with ADHD can't learn and communicate, it is just harder for them. It might take them longer to learn how to communicate and learn the things they need to know.

CONCLUSION

Many people with ADHD don't realize what they're capable of doing until they look back on their lives.

Take note of your good qualities; think about how far you've come and how much you've accomplished. Think about the people you've met and the friends that you've made.

Those who have ADHD often tend to focus on their weaknesses, but it's important that you focus on your strengths.

It's very simple to get wrapped up in the negative aspects of yourself and forget about things that make you a great person. When you focus on your strengths and how amazing you are, it's easier to be happy and make the right decisions.

Spend some time learning from your mistakes and finding out what you could have done differently so that next time, things turn out better. Don't give up when things get tough. Instead, stay positive.

Don't spend time punishing yourself for your mistakes. Instead find the lessons in life that you've learned and what you can do with them to help others. Do your best not to underestimate yourself.

Never focus on punishment because it won't help you in the long run. Learn to forgive yourself because it'll help make you a better person. When you forgive yourself, it's easier to move on and not worry about what has happened in the past.

Find those moments where things went wrong and then think about what you could have done differently. This will help improve your future actions and allow those around you to see a better side of you.

Other people with ADHD have different stories, but they're just as important as yours. It's so simple to get wrapped up in the feeling of being the only one who has this problem, but you're not alone.

Instead of pitying yourself, think about what you can do to help others with ADHD. You may have a hard time relating to others, but it's important that you try to find an individual who understands what you've been through.

Think about how amazing you could be if you tried harder and focused more on your strengths. Instead of being overly critical on yourself, just think about all the lessons that you've learned from your mistakes. You may have learned that you can't change the past, but that doesn't mean that you have to live your life constantly depressed.

Don't complain about your life; instead think about how great it could be if you change some things up. You may have challenges, but they don't have to stay this way for the rest of your life.

It's easy to be pessimistic, but try to look on the brighter side. You may have depression or anxiety, but that doesn't mean that you have to let them rule your life.

Surround yourself with people who are optimistic and do things with a purpose. When you feel good about yourself, you will help others in turn.

You can learn how to control your ADHD so that it doesn't control you. You just need to try your best and take the steps that are necessary to improve yourself. If you do this, then you'll be far happier.

You may not be able to take control what others say about you, but you can control how you react. Choose to smile and think about how amazing everything will be once you learn from your mistakes.

I hope this book helped you with some of your questions. Remember that everyone struggles differently and there's no way to know exactly how you'll react to the challenges you face.

I wish you the best in life, but keep in mind that you've got to work really hard in order to show everyone the great things you can achieve.